Clifton Wilbraham Collins

Saint Simon

Clifton Wilbraham Collins

Saint Simon

ISBN/EAN: 9783337341657

Printed in Europe, USA, Canada, Australia, Japan

Cover: Foto ©Lupo / pixelio.de

More available books at **www.hansebooks.com**

Foreign Classics for English Readers

EDITED BY

MRS OLIPHANT

PROSPECTUS.

THE cordial reception given by the public to the Series of "Ancient Classics for English Readers" has confirmed the intention of the Publishers to carry out a kindred Series, which it is believed will not be less useful or less welcome, and in which an attempt will be made to introduce the great writers of Europe in a similar manner to the many readers who probably have a perfect acquaintance with their names, without much knowledge of their works, or their place in the literature of the modern world. The Classics of Italy, France, Germany, and Spain are nearer to us in time, and less separated in sentiment, than the still more famous Classics of antiquity; and if foreign travel is, as everybody allows, a great means of enlarging the mind, and dispersing its prejudices, an acquaintance with those works in which the great nations who are our neighbours have expressed their highest life, and by which their manners of thinking have been formed, cannot but possess equal advantages. A man who would profess to know England without knowing something of Shakespeare, Bacon, Milton, and the great writers who have followed them, could form but an imperfect idea of the national mind and its capabilities: and so no amount of travel can make us acquainted with Italy, while Dante, Tasso, and her great historians remain unknown to us; nor can the upheavings of French Society and the mental characteristics of the nation be comprehended without Voltaire, Molière, Rousseau, and other great names beside. Neither is Germany herself without Goethe and Schiller: nor Spain recognisable deprived of that noble figure of Cervantes, in whom lives the very genius of the nation. This great band it is our design to give such an account of as may bring them within the acquaintance of the English reader, whose zeal may not carry him the length of the often thankless study of translations, and whose readings in a foreign language are not easy enough to be pleasant. We are aware that there are difficulties in our way in this attempt which did not lie in the path of the former Series, since in the section of the world for which we write there are many more readers of French and German than of Greek and Latin; but, on the other hand, there is no educated class supremely devoted to the study of Continental Classics, as is the case in respect to the Ancient; and even the greatest authority in the learned matter of a Greek text might be puzzled by Jean Paul Richter, or lose himself in the mysteries of Dante's 'Paradiso.' The audience to which we aspire is, therefore, at once wider and narrower than that to which the great treasures of Hellenic and Roman literature are unfamiliar; and our effort will be to present the great Italian, the great Frenchman, the famous German, to the reader, so as to make it plain to him what and how they wrote, something of how they lived, and more or less of their position and influence upon the literature of their country.

The Volumes published of this Series contain—

DANTE,	By the EDITOR.
VOLTAIRE,	By Major-General E. B. HAMLEY.
PASCAL,	By Principal TULLOCH.
PETRARCH,	By HENRY REEVE, C.B.
GOETHE,	By A. HAYWARD, Q.C.
MOLIÈRE,	By Mrs OLIPHANT and F. TARVER, M.A.
MONTAIGNE,	By Rev. W. LUCAS COLLINS, M.A.
RABELAIS,	By WALTER BESANT.
CALDERON,	By E. J. HASELL.
SAINT SIMON,	By CLIFTON W. COLLINS, M.A.

Volumes in preparation—

CERVANTES,	By the EDITOR.
MADAME DE SÉVIGNE AND MADAME DE STAEL,	By Miss THACKERAY.

Foreign Classics for English Readers

EDITED BY

MRS OLIPHANT

SAINT SIMON

BY
CLIFTON W. COLLINS, M. A.

PHILADELPHIA:
J. B. LIPPINCOTT & CO.
1880.

CONTENTS.

CHAP.		PAGE
I.	INTRODUCTION,	1
II.	SAINT SIMON'S FAMILY,	24
III.	SAINT SIMON IN THE ARMY,	30
IV.	VERSAILLES,	42
V.	PRINCES AND PRINCESSES,	57
VI.	MADAME DE MAINTENON,	66
VII.	SAINT SIMON'S LIFE AT COURT,	84
VIII.	JESUITS AND JANSENISTS,	99
IX.	THE SPANISH SUCCESSION,	122
X.	THE PROVINCES,	136
XI.	MEUDON AND MONSEIGNEUR,	144
XII.	THE DUKE AND DUCHESS OF BURGUNDY,	155
XIII.	THE LAST DAYS OF LOUIS XIV.,	168
XIV.	THE REGENT,	183
XV.	CARDINAL DUBOIS,	199
XVI.	SAINT SIMON IN RETIREMENT,	213

SAINT SIMON.

CHAPTER I.

INTRODUCTION.

"A SECRET historian; a geometrician, diseased in body and mind; a good easy man, always dreaming, and treated as a dreamer,—there you have the three artists of the seventeenth century. They have startled and perhaps a little shocked us all. La Fontaine, the happiest, was the most perfect; Pascal, Christian and philosopher, the most elevated; Saint Simon, given up entirely to his fancy, is the most powerful and the most true."[1] This is high praise, coming as it does from an accomplished critic like M. Taine, and must sound strange to many who know little of Saint Simon beyond the fact that he wrote memoirs of Louis XIV.'s reign. Most of the great writers of that age are familiar names enough to us. La Fontaine's Fables, Pascal's 'Pensées,' Fénelon's 'Télémaque,' the plays of Molière and Racine,

[1] Taine, Essais, p. 297.

the sermons of Bossuet and Bourdaloue, and the letters of Madame de Sévigné, have their place in most libraries; and, even in the form of selections or extracts, have probably been read to some extent by most persons who have read French at all. But Saint Simon, whose genius was in its own way as remarkable as theirs, and who has given us in his incomparable Memoirs a living picture of the old *régime*, is still, we believe, almost unknown, except to the historian or reviewer. To ordinary readers in this country he is still the shadow of a name, and nothing more. Even if we do not go so far as to ask, as some literary lady once asked, "Why was he made a saint?" he is not unfrequently confused with his namesake and descendant, the Saint Simon of revolutionary fame; and the philosophic friend of Robespierre is credited with having written the memoirs of his ancestor—the aristocrat of aristocrats.

At the same time it is not surprising that Saint Simon should be so little read. The fact is, that between the pressure of business and the whirl of modern society, few men have time to read anything beyond the reviews and periodicals of the day—if indeed they can find time to read so much; and supposing that, in a fit of self-improvement, they take some classic from their bookshelves, or turn back to the literature of the eighteenth century, the last book that they would be likely to select would be a set of French memoirs in twenty volumes, digressive and discursive, and difficult to follow from the obscurity of the style and the variety of contemporary allusions. But the great drawback in his case (and it is the one unpardonable sin in a writer) is his length. Even Macaulay, who was credited with reading Photius for pleasure, confesses that he found Saint Simon wearisome. "The good parts," he declared, on reading the Memoirs a second time, "were as good as ever, but the road from fountain to fountain lay through a very dry desert." An ordinary reader may well be excused for shrinking from a task that tried Macaulay's patience; indeed it may be doubted if any one in this generation (excepting perhaps Saint Simon's learned editor, M. Chéruel) has ever even tried to wade through those long and dreary chapters describing the ceremonial of the Spanish Court, the different classes of Spanish grandees, and the exact position and privileges of the French dukes and the Parliament of Paris. These tedious digressions spring from a weakness inherent in Saint Simon's character— his mania for all questions connected with rank and pedigrees of the nobility. He seems indeed to have had the whole French peerage by heart. All their titles and dignities were intensely interesting to him; and he takes a singular delight in tracing the exact family history and relationship of nearly every personage he mentions in his Memoirs. The Baron Von-Thunder-Ten-Tronckh himself could not have been more exacting; and if there is a blot in any one of the "seize quartiers" of the family coat of arms, Saint Simon is sure to put his finger on it. For example, when the Abbé de Soubise was about to be received into the Chapter of Strasburg, Saint Simon at once goes back to the Abbé's great-grandmother. Who was *she*? "A daughter of that cook, formerly scullion, and afterwards lackey to Henry IV.!" Again, when the Princess des Ursins' brother was about to make what was thought a *mésalliance*, Saint Simon writes: "Madame des Ursins cried out as if their own mother had not been Aubry, their grandmother Bouhier daughter of the treasurer of a savings-bank, and their great-grandmother Beaune." So too, when Cardinal Alberoni wrote in a grand style of his dignity as a Roman citizen, and talked of "our Tacitus"—"A *Roman*, forsooth!" says Saint Simon; "why, he belonged to a little village near Bayonne, where his father sold cabbages, and he wormed himself into favour by making cheese-salads for Vendôme." Even the "affaire du bonnet," to which Saint Simon points again and again, as if it involved the gravest constitutional principles, was really only a trivial question of etiquette — whether the President should wear his cap on his head or place it before him on the table, when he addressed the peers in Parliament.

As we shall find, during the first few years of his life at Court he was incessantly occupied in trying these questions of precedence, and in questioning the genuineness of some of the proudest titles in France. It seems, on the face of it, a little absurd that a young duke of recent creation (for Saint Simon was only the second who bore the title) should be continually taking up arms against "new men"—or "mushrooms of fortune," as he terms them; but this firm belief in his own order—*morgue aristocratique*—is the key-note to his political career as well as to his character. The more he studied history, he tells us, the more firmly he was convinced that it was the dukes, and the dukes alone, who should or could save France in the future, as they had saved her in the past. Mischief enough had already been done during "the long reign of the *vil bourgeois*," and it was the peers, with the dukes at their head, who should direct the councils of their sovereign.

In fact, Saint Simon would have revived the aristocracy of the feudal system, which had perished some centuries before he was born, and have transferred the institutions of Philip Augustus to the reign of Louis XIV. We shall find that in all his political schemes, both in connection with the young Duke of Burgundy and with the Regent Orleans, he constantly reverted to this ideal constitution,—a hierarchy culminating in the ducal rank, raised far above the lower orders of nobility, and having its place on the steps of the throne itself. This day-dream —for it was nothing more—had a special fascination for him, and he alludes to it in a hundred scattered passages; but it is almost unnecessary to add, that of all the wild and fanciful schemes ever imagined by philosopher or politician, this was perhaps the wildest and most hopelessly impossible.

Saint Simon either looked back to the past, or he looked forward to the future. Of the present time, and of the men of his own generation, he always speaks with the utmost bitterness. Society—that is, the Court, as he saw it—seemed to consist chiefly of rogues and rascals (*fripons et scélérats*), and, generally speaking, the most successful were in his eyes the greatest scoundrels. On whichever side he looked, he could find nothing but the vilest passions, the meanest motives, the basest principles; men employing their lives in some miserable intrigue for some miserable object—wasting their talents and squandering their fortunes, and supplanting their neighbours by superior villany. And of all detestable characters, he paints in the strongest colours those of unprincipled priests like Dubois and Le Tellier, and unscrupulous lawyers like Harlay and Maisons

Of a few intimate personal friends he speaks in terms of almost unqualified praise. Nothing is too good for his spiritual adviser, La Trappe; for his father-in-law, Marshal Lorges; for his friend and confidant, the Duke of Beauvilliers; and for his young hero, the Duke of Burgundy. But such men were as the very salt of the earth—the few good grains among the host of tares—and their solitary virtues only heightened the contrast of the corruption and profligacy around them. The strange thing is, that Saint Simon singles out for special attack precisely those men who were among the most distinguished and esteemed of their own generation. Among them we find such names as Noailles, the gay and fortunate diplomatist; Antin, the most charming and versatile of courtiers; Vendôme, the idol of the army, and the prince of boon companions; Villars, the hero of fifty battles; Rochefoucauld, the type of a *grand seigneur*. These men are each in their turn branded by Saint Simon with every epithet of scorn and hatred, and held up by him to everlasting ridicule. We have only to refer to the marginal summaries drawn up by his own hands, and we find that he has almost exhausted the vocabulary of abuse in describing their characters. Wickedness, perfidy, avarice, monstrous ingratitude, hateful obstinacy, criminal folly, faults upon faults, are some of the phases applied by him to the statesmen and soldiers of his time; and he describes the Duc de Noailles—who, if we may believe his apologist, has as much claim to our respect as Saint Simon himself—as "the most faithful and the most perfect copy of the serpent that tempted Eve,—so far as a man can approach the qualities of the chief of the fallen angels."

But even this language is mild and moderate compared with that which he employs in describing such men as Vendôme and Dubois, or such women as the Regent's daughter, whom he seems to have hated with the perfect hatred of the old covenant. It is then that his indignation masters him, and his language becomes Scriptural in the vehemence of his denunciation. Indeed, we know of nothing since the days of the second Philippic so bitter, so scathing and so incisive, except perhaps Junius's indictment of the Duke of Grafton, or Macaulay's description of Barère.

In Saint Simon's case, time, instead of softening, seems only to have embittered the unrelenting hostility with which he pursues his enemies through their lives and after their deaths—

" Eternal as their own, his hate
　Surmounts the bounds of mortal fate,
　And dies not with the dead."

He dwells with an irrepressible satisfaction upon every incident in their decline and fall. He gloats over the closing scenes in their career, and he draws from their history the solemn warning of guilt followed by its attendant punishment, which, like the Nemesis or Até of the Greek drama, strikes down the insolent and guilty wretch in the very plenitude of his triumph. He is not surprised at the awful fate that befell the rich and learned Maisons, and destroyed him and his family through three generations. Such destruction was only the fitting reward of his impiety. So again, when the Bishop of Soissons died suddenly and terribly,—it was the judgment of God on him, says Saint Simon, for having sold himself to the Jesuits, and for having signed the " Constitution."

History, he thought, was full of such moral lessons to him who read it as it should be read; and to give due effect to these lessons was part of the duty of the historian. "To him who considers the events which history records in their real and first origin, their degrees, and their progress, there is perhaps no religious book—next to Holy Scripture itself, and the great book of nature always open before our eyes—which so greatly raises our thoughts to God, which so continually keeps us in wonder and astonishment, or which shows us so clearly our nothingness and our blindness."

But while he had this exalted idea of the purpose of history, he never seems to have realised his own responsibility as a historian. He wrote always furiously and recklessly—neither weighing his words nor measuring the effect of his sweeping denunciations of the men and society of his time. Generally speaking, a writer is induced to measure his statements and qualify his opinions by the ordinary restraints of publicity and criticism: "to-morrow the critics will come," and it is the fear of this "to-morrow," and of its pains and penalties, that acts as a safeguard against rash attacks on personal reputations. But the man who writes, as Saint Simon wrote, in the secrecy of his chamber, conscious that, in his time, no eye but his own will ever see his manuscripts; and knowing, as he knew, that his work will only be read when he is himself far beyond the reach of praise or censure,—such a man writes without scruple or responsibility, with the curb loosened from his tongue and with the bridle taken off his lips. There can be no action for libel with the dead; friends and foes will be equally powerless to defend or attack him; the verdict of posterity—whatever that verdict may be—can never reach him; and his fame will come, if it comes at all, from a generation that never knew him.

"Son laurier tardif n'ombrage que sa tombe."

Such a writer will be free to indulge in all the luxury of scorn and invective, to gratify every personal pique, to avenge himself on those who have insulted and injured him in his lifetime, by leaving them in their turn pilloried for ever in a fool's paradise. And it is of this easy and not very dignified method of attack and retaliation that St Simon has undoubtedly availed himself. He has left his Memoirs behind him, as a mine is left in a deserted fortress, on the chance of an explosion that may ruin and destroy the enemy. This is what Chateaubriand meant when he said that "Saint Simon écrit à la diable pour l'immortalité!"

As a matter of fact, Saint Simon dared no more have published his Memoirs in his own lifetime, than the author of 'Junius' dared to drop his mask. We can fancy the storm of indignation that would have broken out, when the noblest families in France found themselves traduced and maligned by this "little man-devouring duke," as Argenson called him; when the Jesuits found worse things said of their Order by their supposed friend than had ever been said of them by their avowed enemy, Pascal; when his colleagues in office found their abilities disparaged and their policy assailed by the man whom they regarded with some justice as the most incompetent politician of their number. " If these Memoirs ever see the light," wrote their author, "I doubt not that they will cause a prodigious revulsion of feeling;" and it was fortunate for his personal safety that no accident ever betrayed their existence to his own generation. He would certainly have found himself in the Bastille before many days had passed — already being, as is proved by the songs and lampoons of the time, probably the most unpopular man in France. That he was himself fully sensible of the risk he ran is shown by his intense anxiety that some papers he had lent the Duke of Burgundy should not fall into the king's hands. "A writer who writes the truth, and nothing but the truth, must have lost his senses," he says, "if he allows it even to be suspected that he is writing. His work ought to be guarded by keys and the surest bolts, and to pass thus guarded to his heirs after him, who in their turn would do wisely to let it abide for one or two generations, and not to let it see the light till time has buried all resentments."

The difficulty that meets us on the threshold of his Memoirs is what to believe and what not to believe. Knowing how genuine and sincere Saint Simon is even in his hatreds, we should be disposed to accept all he has told us with implicit confidence. But then, unfortunately, we find his authority on so many matters of fact discredited, and in some cases disproved, by contemporary witnesses, that considerable suspicion rests on these countless anecdotes and *bons histoires* scattered through his pages. Some of these stories, so gravely recounted by him, are as wonderful in their way as anything that Herodotus heard from the Egyptian priests; indeed, since the days of the Father of History, it would be difficult to find another writer so inquisitive, so credulous, and so garrulously-given as Saint Simon. We cannot say that his stories are not true, because he is often the only writer who has recorded them, and we have no means of proving either their truth or falsehood. But presumptive evidence is in many instances against them, and leaves us no alternative but to class them with those delightful stories of our childhood that enlivened the dreariest narratives, — Clarence's Malmsey butt, Tell's apple, Cambronne's famous speech, Louis XVI.'s last words — what Mommsen calls "the rubbish-heap of tradition," or what Mr Hayward places among "the mock pearls of history."

When, for instance, Saint Simon tells us of the farrier of Salon and the marvellous vision that he saw, and how he told it to the king, and what the king said of it; or of the magpie that appeared to La Varenne, and its miraculous speech, and how La Varenne at once took to his bed and died,—all this reads like the headings of chapters from the "Morte d'Arthur." So, again, when he describes so graphically how Marshal Villars was left alone under the tree at Friedlingen, weeping and tearing his hair for the battle that he believed lost, but was really all the time won by his lieutenant,—the description is as grotesque, and probably about as true, as Juvenal's picture of the one-eyed Hannibal riding on the last of his elephants. In the same way the hunting adventure that led to the death of Fargues, so dramatically told,— the story of the black princess who lived in a convent, and was thought to be some great personage ("*fort énigmatique*," says Saint Simon) — the poisoning of Henrietta of Orleans—the secret marriage of Cardinal

Dubois—the pathetic death of Racine of a broken heart, —all these romantic tales must, we fear, be consigned to the same borderland between fact and fiction as the legends of ancient Rome or the historical plays of Shakespeare. But which is fact and which is fiction in this region of uncertainties, it is not within the province of this volume to determine. We must take Saint Simon as we find him, and, unless he is clearly and flagrantly wrong, leave him the responsibility of his own stories.

It is a pity that there should be even a question of doubt in his case, — that a writer with all his keenness of observation and marvellous powers of description, with almost every faculty needed to make a great historian, should fail in the one essential point — historical truth. In this respect his very talents have been a snare to him. His fondness for anything graphic and picturesque, his appreciation of a good story when he heard one (and we can trace this taste in the countless *bon mots* and anecdotes that he regales us with), his eagerness always to point the moral and adorn the tale, when he had the chance of doing so,—all this inclined him to take the picturesque and poetical side of what he saw and heard, rather than confine himself to the dull and prosaic region of commonplace.

Again, Saint Simon seems to have been wanting in another gift, necessary to the man who tells us the history of his times—the capacity for examining and sifting evidence. He evidently believed implicitly whatever his friends chose to tell him; indeed he is candid enough to give us several instances in which Orleans or Lauzun practised on his credulity, and we can well believe that these were not solitary exceptions. "My character," he says, "upright, frank, free, natural, and far too simple, was expressly made for being taken in the snares." All the gossip of the back-stairs, all the scandalous stories that circulated in the Œil de Bœuf or on the terraces of Marly, all the ill-natured tales told him by his brother-in-law, Lauzun, whom he declares to be a perfect treasury of anecdotes,—Saint Simon heard and duly noted down evening after evening. Then again, he constantly cross-questioned the king's surgeon and the king's valets —much as Mr Greville cross-questioned old Batchelor— and we may imagine that what he heard in this way did not lose in the transmission. But it was just this kind of information, got in this underhand manner, that he considers, as he is careful to tell us, the most important and valuable of all testimony. These men, he says, —Bontems, and Bloin, and Maréchal—were always in the royal bedroom or presence-chamber, and were all eyes and ears.

He frequently describes interviews, in his dramatic fashion, which could not possibly have been known to more than two or three people, and which, it might be supposed, would have been kept profoundly secret by them —for their own safety and reputation, if for no other reason. But nothing seems to have been hidden from this keen and vigilant observer. He was as ubiquitous and omniscient as those scandalmongers described by Plautus;[1] and even the circumstances of a *tête-à-tête* in the king's private cabinet or the Regent's bedroom seem, by some means or other, to have reached Saint Simon's ears. To take an instance at random: we are told how "Monsieur's" first wife—Henrietta, daughter of Charles

[1] Plautus, Trinummus, i. 2.

I. of England—died suddenly and terribly, in the prime of her youth and beauty, in 1670, after only a few hours' illness. Bossuet has painted for us, in a famous sermon, the confusion and terror at Versailles when the Court was awaked at midnight by the cry of "*Madame se meurt,*" and then of "*Madame est morte;*" and Saint Simon gives, in his own manner, what was probably the popular version of her death. The king, who was greatly shocked by what had happened, suspected foul play on the part of some of the dissolute hangers-on in Monsieur's household, and before dawn the same morning sent for Brissac, lieutenant of his guards:—

"He told him to choose six body-guards, trusty men, whose secrecy could be depended on, and send them to seize the house-steward, and bring him to his cabinet by the backstairs. This was done before daybreak. As soon as the king perceived him, he ordered Brissac and the chief valet to retire, and putting on a countenance and tone likely to cause the greatest terror—

"'My friend,' said he, looking at the man from head to foot, 'listen to me carefully: if you confess everything, and only answer the truth in what I wish to know,—whatever you have done, I pardon you, and the matter shall never be mentioned. But take care not to conceal the least thing from me, for if you do so, you are a dead man before you leave the room. Has Madame been poisoned?'

"'Yes, Sire,' he answered.

"'And who has poisoned her, and how was it done?'

"He replied that it was the Chevalier de Lorraine who had sent the poison to Beuvron and to Effiat, and told the king all I have just written. Then the king, redoubling his assurance of pardon and his menaces of death—

"'And my brother, did *he* know?'

"'No, Sire; none of us three were fools enough to tell

him about it. He can never keep a secret: he would have ruined us all.'

"At this answer the king gave a great 'Ha!' like a man oppressed by a weight, and who all at once breathes again.

"'Very well,' said he, 'that is all I wanted to know. But are you positive of what you say? Do you assure me distinctly it is so?'

"He then called back Brissac, and ordered him to escort the man part of his way, when all at once he let him go at liberty."

The whole scene is probably a fiction, for there is the clearest evidence that the Princess Henrietta was not poisoned at all; but it illustrates so well Saint Simon's manner of treating a story that interested him, that we have given it just as it stands. Most writers would have contented themselves with recording the fact that Louis was supposed to have sent for his brother's steward and wrung a confession from him; but Saint Simon tells it all as dramatically as if he had been himself hidden behind the tapestry, and heard every word that passed in this strange interview. And it is the same throughout the Memoirs. Wherever he can, he throws his narrative into the form of a dialogue, and these dialogues are so real and lifelike, that, excepting in Balzac and Walter Scott, we know of nothing like them in romance or history. We should have been inclined to have classed them with the fictitious speeches in Livy or Thucydides; but Saint Simon claims for them a far higher authenticity. They are, he expressly says, the faithful reports of actual speeches, written *sur le champ*, and losing rather than gaining in effect by being written instead of spoken. And as far as his own speeches are concerned, we can quite imagine that the fire and force of his natural eloquence could scarcely be reproduced in writing, especially in some of his stormy interviews with Noailles and the Regent, where the concentrated passion of the speaker breathes through every line of his remonstrance or invective, and makes one almost regret that he could not have lived a century later and enlivened a modern parliamentary debate.

Among the critics of his own country, from Voltaire downwards, Saint Simon has found nearly as many enemies as friends. Both the Duc de Noailles and M. Theophile Lavallée pronounce his personal prejudices to be stronger than his sense of truth; M. Monty has written an essay to show that he was sour and cross-grained in character; M. Chéruel, in his learned work, tells us that he is prejudiced, inconsistent, partial, credulous, and a fabulist rather than a historian. But, on the other hand, there is another school of critics, beginning with Villemain and Marmontel, who have set him on a pinnacle above every other prose writer of his time. By these admirers he is declared to be caustic as Le Sage, pathetic as Racine, picturesque as Tacitus. Taine, as has been seen, ranks him with Pascal and La Fontaine; and Sainte Beuve places him alongside of Bossuet and Molière. Praise cannot go much beyond this; still, it is worth while quoting the great critic's last panegyric on his favourite author:—

" You talk of Tacitus, who has admirably condensed, worked up, kneaded, cooked and recooked at the [midnight] lamp, who has gilded with a sombre tint his burning and bitter pictures,—do not repent, Frenchmen, of having had among you in the heart of Court life at Versailles, and ever on the track of the human quarry, this little duke with the piercing eye, cruel, insatiable, always on the chase, ferreting about present everywhere, swooping on his prey, and laying waste on all sides. Thanks to him,—a Tacitus with natural humour and with unbridled fancy,—we have nothing to envy in the earlier writer. And what is more, the vein of comedy, which he has so boldly scattered through his Memoirs, has given us in him a Tacitus *à la Shakespeare.*"[1]

It only remains to say something as to the history of these famous Memoirs,—how they were originally written, and how they have descended to us. As is well known, Saint Simon amused himself in his old age by making notes in an interleaved copy of Dangeau's Memoirs, but it may be doubted whether (as has been thought) "he condescended to borrow from Dangeau by a curious kind of plagiarism."[2] The two writers had absolutely nothing in common beyond the fact that their memoirs related to the same period; and they differed so entirely in their method and their manner of treating the same subjects, that they cannot even be compared. It may be safely said that, if anything, Dangeau owes far more to Saint Simon than Saint Simon owes to Dangeau; for the only readable portions of those twenty octavo volumes, which M. Feuillet de Conches has so laboriously edited, are the notes and illustrations added by Saint Simon. Dangeau's Memoirs themselves are as dull and uninteresting as pages from the 'Court Circular' or the 'London Gazette.' "The king took medicine;" "Monseigneur went out wolf-hunting;" "Madame passed the afternoon with Mademoiselle Bessola;"—and so on, page after page, and volume after volume. "It is difficult," as Saint Simon says, "to understand how a man could

---

[1] Sainte Beuve, Nouveaux Lundis, x. 263.
[2] Reeve's Royal and Republican France, i. 126.

have had the patience and perseverance to write a work like this every day for fifty years—so dry, so meagre, so constrained, and so literally matter-of-fact."

Nor again does it seem clear, as many editors suppose, that Saint Simon's "additions" to Dangeau's Memoirs were the basis of his own; indeed it may be questioned whether he even thought of annotating Dangeau's Memoirs till his own were in a fair way of completion. He tells us expressly that it was his reading the memoirs of the last century that first suggested the idea of his writing his own; that he began his journal in 1694, when he was a young lieutenant encamped with Marshal Lorges's army on the Rhine. In 1699, again, we find him writing to the Abbot of La Trappe, to ask his advice (as he always did) in a matter of conscience. He has been writing memoirs, he tells La Trappe, of which "a considerable part is finished," and in which "the reputations of thousands of people are compromised;" and he asks for some rule by which he can speak the truth without wounding his conscience. What answer was returned we have no means of knowing; but as Saint Simon sent him his account of the Luxemburg lawsuit,[1] La Trappe had the opportunity, at any rate, of forming an opinion as to the tone and spirit of the remainder.

In any case, from that time until 1723 (nearly thirty years) Saint Simon continued day after day, or rather evening after evening, secretly taking notes of all that passed before him,—even writing down the actual words of the speeches used. After some striking scene at Court—that after Monseigneur's death, for instance,

[1] See p. 35.

which Sainte Beuve pronounces to be unrivalled in history—he would sit in his dark cabinet at the back of his suite of rooms, writing fast and furiously, without resting to polish or correct, careless as to whether his sentences were incoherent or the style confused, so long as the picture itself stood out boldly from the canvas. What cared he for "style"? He owns himself that he never regarded his manner of expression, so long as he could explain his meaning.

"I was never a student of the Academy. I have not been able to cure myself of the fault of writing rapidly. To make my style more exact and agreeable by correcting it, would be to recast the whole work, and this labour would pass my strength, and would run the risk of being unpleasing (*ingrat*). To correct well what one has written, one must know how to write well. It will be easily seen that I have no right to pique myself on *that* quality. I have thought of nothing all along except exactitude and truth."

For thirty years, as has been said, Saint Simon continued to write daily his impressions of men and events as they passed before him, and then, when he finally left the Court in 1723, he carried with him this enormous mass of notes and memoranda and treatises and essays; and these were the rough materials of his Memoirs, as well as of the notes and illustrations copied by him into the blank pages of Dangeau's journal. For thirteen years he continued this work of revision and selection. Then, lastly, in 1740, he began to make a fair copy of the whole,—transcribing them carefully in a small clear hand, with many abbreviations, but few corrections. Even thus written closely, they filled three thousand folio sheets. Following the example of Buffon and

Bossuet, he divided them into neither volumes nor chapters, but added a marginal summary, and a classified index of subjects.

Thus the Memoirs were really the one engrossing occupation of his lifetime,—not of the few years preceding his death.

Saint Simon, with all his talents, was the worst possible man of business ("I scarcely know the four simple rules of arithmetic," he told the Regent, when he wanted to make him Minister of Finance), and he died heavily in debt. By his will he left his manuscripts to his cousin, the Bishop of Metz, as being a man of prudence and discretion, and an exact inventory was made of them accordingly. But the creditors claimed them, and a lawsuit took place between them and the heirs of the estate, to decide the right of possession,—the latter wanting to keep them as heirlooms, and the former to realise something by their sale. It ended, however, in a higher authority intervening; and all these precious documents, after having been left six years in charge of M. Delaleu, a notary, were impounded and carried off to the Foreign Office "by order of the king." So far this was an advantage, as it prevented their being dispersed or sold: in fact, M. Baschet thinks their seizure may have been the result of a secret agreement between Saint Simon's family and the Duke de Choiseul, the Foreign Minister.

It was evidently known from the first, that among these numerous manuscript volumes (about 280 in all), these famous Memoirs might be found; for, shortly after they had been locked up in the Foreign Office, we find the Abbé de Voisenon commissioned to read them and extract some of the more piquant anecdotes to amuse Louis XV. and Madame de Pompadour; and Madame du Deffand wrote in 1771 to Horace Walpole that she had just read them "with inexpressible delight," and promised to send them to him by the hands of a certain Abbé. But they underwent "a strange adventure" on their way from Chanteloup, and never reached Strawberry Hill. Though still kept "prisoners of state," it seems that they were lent from time to time to certain privileged persons, and copies, all more or less incorrect, made from the more interesting portions. Voltaire had seen them, and intended to refute them. Duclos used them for his 'Secret History of Louis XIV.,' and Marmontel (and Anquetil after him) made large extracts from them.

In 1780 a volume was published at Brussels, purporting to be extracts from the journal of a celebrated duke and man of letters, "better known by the excess of his frankness than by that of his credulity." Then appeared 'A Gallery of the Ancient Court;' and at last, in 1788, Saint Simon's name was boldly placed on the title-page of some extracts from the Memoirs, borrowed or stolen by one Soulavie, who seems to have been as impudent and as unscrupulous an impostor as La Beaumelle. But all this time the precious Memoirs themselves remained with the rest of the manuscripts in the Foreign Office, and it was not till 1819 that the head of the family (a General Saint Simon) obtained leave from Louis XVIII. to have his ancestor's journals handed over to him. In 1830 the first authentic and complete edition was published, and it was at the meeting of the Sorbonne in the same year that Villemain pronounced his well-known panegyric on the writer. We are told the effect produced on the literary world at Paris by their publication was prodigious, and Sainte Beuve can only compare it to that caused by the Waverley Novels. It was, he says, as if a curtain had suddenly been lifted from the past century, and had let in a flood of light upon every corner of Versailles as it might be seen in the days of the Great King.

The Memoirs, as we have them now in M. Chéruel's edition, leave nothing to be desired in the way of completeness and correctness, but they are not a tenth part of what Saint Simon actually wrote and left behind him. There are still to be found, buried somewhere in the catacombs of the Foreign Office on the Quay d'Orsay, no less than two hundred and sixty-six portfolios or volumes filled with notes, letters, treatises, and memoranda, all in Saint Simon's handwriting. All these documents had been kept together until M. Dumont classified and rearranged the archives of the Foreign Office in 1848. Where they are now, no one seems exactly to know. They appear to be regarded in the light of an "Eleusinian mystery," about which it is a sacrilege even to inquire; and the questions asked from time to time by some inquisitive man of letters are not only not answered, but produce "an emotion" in the official mind. When Guizot was Foreign Minister, an attempt was made towards publishing some of the State papers of the Monarchy, and we have the result in Mignet's work on the 'Spanish Succession.' Had he only added to this the publication of Saint Simon's 'Paquet d'Espagne,' some further new and curious light might have been thrown on the tangled web of diplomacy which preceded the great war.

It is impossible even to conjecture what is or what is not contained in this mass of unpublished manuscripts. Lemontey says that among them is an "immense and varied correspondence"—nearly nine hundred letters—probably the original of every letter Saint Simon received, and the copy of every letter he wrote. These would no doubt explain much that is obscure and inconsistent in the Memoirs. They might rectify his injustices; they might give reasons for his unaccountable prejudices; they might possibly reveal a kindliness and good-nature unsuspected at present; they might give us the genial and domestic side of his character. In short, until his letters are published, we cannot be said to know Saint Simon.[1] Whether they will ever be published or not depends on the liberality or caprice of the French Foreign Office; but so many literary men have so often vainly tried even to get a sight of these famous manuscripts, that not much hope of success is given for the future. The worst fear is that their publication may be delayed until it is too late,— that some accidental fire, or some fresh outburst of Communism, may destroy these priceless manuscripts, and that they may be as irrecoverably lost to posterity as the missing decades of Livy or the greater part of the orations of Lysias.[2]

[1] "Un Saint Simon épistolaire et prime-sautier est tout entier à révéler."—Baschet.

[2] It appears that the permission, so long sought for, has at last been given (March 1880),—thanks to M. de Freycinet, Minister for Foreign Affairs,—and that M. de Beilisle is preparing a new edition of the Memoirs, while M. Drumont is studying the documents connected with Saint Simon's embassy to Spain in 1721.

CHAPTER II.

SAINT SIMON'S FAMILY.

LA FERTÉ VIDAME, Saint Simon's family seat, where the Rouvroys had lived from time immemorial, was a feudal chateau, built in a square, and guarded by a moat and embattled walls. Of the chateau itself not a stone remains. Not many years after Saint Simon's death it was bought by the great capitalist Jean Joseph Laborde, who, with all his good qualities, had certainly no antiquarian tastes, for he destroyed the old chateau with its traditions and associations, and built in its stead a house in a more modern style. But though the chateau itself has disappeared, such an exact inventory of its contents has been left among Saint Simon's papers, that we know every picture and piece of tapestry in each room; the chairs covered with brocaded silk; the curtains of green *taffetas* with gold fringe; the library of six thousand volumes; and even the writing-table " of cherrywood, covered with stamped morocco," on which the famous Memoirs were written, and the "bureau with seven drawers," where they were probably kept under lock and key.

Claude Saint Simon, father of the Memoir-writer, had

been a page in the Court of Louis XIII., and owed his fortune to a lucky accident. The king, like all the Bourbons, was passionately fond of hunting, and it was part of Claude Saint Simon's duties to bring him his second horse; and his ingenuity in enabling his Majesty to change horses without dismounting was his first introduction to the royal favour. Once started at Court, the little page of the stables rose by rapid steps. He became Chief Squire, First Gentleman of the Bedchamber, Grand Wolf-hunter, Knight of the Order of the Holy Ghost, Captain of the Palace-Guard at Saint Germains, and Governor of the Castle of Blaye. Throughout his description Saint Simon paints his father as the Last of the Barons—"one in whom some spark of the feudal spirit still burned"—the hero of a bygone age and "the devoted servant of the best and greatest of kings." We are told that his sagacity and discretion made him many friends at Court, and even gained for him the confidence of the great Richelieu himself.

"When the shades of misfortune were gathering round this Minister," says Saint Simon, "my father was often suddenly awoke at midnight by his bed-curtains being drawn aside by a valet with a candlestick in his hand, and there would be Richelieu standing behind him. And the cardinal would then take the candlestick and seat himself at the foot of the bed, crying out that he was lost, and had come to my father for advice and assistance, repeating some orders he had received, or some passage of arms that he had just had with the king."

In fact, it was by Claude Saint Simon's help that Richelieu, on the eve of his disgrace, had the long secret interview with Louis, and rehearsed the farce of his pretended resignation, to be afterwards publicly performed on the celebrated " Day of Dupes." By Louis himself Saint Simon was both honoured and trusted, and all would have gone well with him (if we may believe his son) had he not incurred the enmity of Chavigny, the Minister of War. On some affront, real or fancied, from this Minister, he threw up his office at Court, and retired to the Castle of Blaye. There he stayed some four years, still keeping up a correspondence with Louis, until summoned once more to Versailles on the occasion of the king's last illness. It was his duty at the funeral to throw the sword of state upon the coffin as it lay in the open vault, and, says Saint Simon, "he has often told me that, when he threw the sword, he was for the moment on the point of throwing himself after it."

In that grave lay buried the hero and idol of the old duke's life; and the memory of Louis XIII. was always kept sacred at the chateau of La Ferté. Saint Simon himself wore a ring with this king's miniature set in diamonds on it; there was a picture of him in every room both of his town and country houses; there was a statue of him in the chapel, with a lamp kept constantly burning before it.

"Never," says Saint Simon, " did my father console himself for the death of Louis XIII.; never did he speak of him without tears in his eyes; never did he mention him except as the king his master; never did he fail going to Saint Denis on his behalf, year after year, on the 14th of May, or to offer to his memory a solemn mass at Blaye when he found himself there on that anniversary. It was a feeling of veneration, affectionate remembrance, even tenderness, that he expressed in words whenever he spoke of him; and he gloried in dwelling upon his personal exploits and on his private virtues."

Saint Simon's account of the heroic part played by his father in the war of the Fronde has been called in question, with some reason. It is even said to be almost entirely pure romance; but we must leave the responsibility of his statements with the writer. According to his account, nothing could be nobler or more independent than the duke's conduct in those troubled times which followed Louis XIII.'s death. He resisted all the tempting offers of Condé; he refused the bribes of the King of Spain; he was proof even against the charming eloquence of the Duchess de Longueville; he armed 500 gentlemen at his own expense, and garrisoned Blaye in the name of the King of France; and when proposals came for a surrender of the place, he threatened to tie a shot to the heels of the next messenger and throw him into the Gironde,—" for as long as he lived," he said, " he would never fail the child and widow of his old master." In gratitude Mazarin offered him the choice of a marshal's baton or the title of prince; but the old duke, in his pride, would have neither the one nor the other. He would never, he declared, tarnish the honour of his family by allowing it to be supposed possible that his loyalty could be bought or sold.

Some years after this, Claude Saint Simon happened one day to look into Rochefoucauld's Memoirs of his Time, and there found himself represented as having broken his word to Condé, and holding Blaye for the king, when he had agreed to surrender it to the Frondists.

"My father felt so keenly the atrocity of this calumny that he seized a pen and wrote on the margin of the volume, '*The writer has told a lie.*' Not content with this, he then went and discovered the publisher (for the book was not sold openly on its first appearance), and asked to see all the copies of the work,—prayed, promised, threatened, and was so persistent that he made the man show them. He at once took a pen and wrote in every copy the same marginal note as before. You may imagine the astonishment of the bookseller and the subsequent indignation of M. de Rochefoucauld. There was a great noise made in the matter, but nothing came of it."

The old duke married again in 1670—a charming wife—and soon afterwards there came a letter from Madame de Montespan, offering to the new duchess what was then supposed a high mark of Court favour, the post of Lady-in-Waiting to the king's mistress. But the duke would not hear of it. "He opened the letter, and at once took a pen and politely declined the offer, adding, that 'at his age he had taken a wife, not for the Court, but for himself.'"

The writer of the Memoirs was the child of the second marriage, being born in 1675; and he always speaks of his mother, on the few occasions when he mentions her name, in terms of affection and respect, although he does not think it necessary to go into her family history. "She was an Aubefine,"—he says, very curtly; and one is inclined to suspect that the Aubefines had not much to boast of in the way of pedigree, and certainly could not be compared to his father's family, the Rouvroys, who traced their descent from Charlemagne. But though, after the first few chapters, the dowager-duchess disappears from the Memoirs, she seems to have indirectly exercised a strong influence over her son. Even when he was fifty years old, and a member of the Regent's Council, we find him still deferring to her authority, although the question was the marriage of his daughter. The rest of the family, including the young lady herself, were strongly opposed to the match; yet he tells us, "My mother thought differently, and she was accustomed to decide." And the marriage took place as she wished.

Among other pieces of good advice that his mother gave him during his boyhood was a warning that his future in life must depend on himself, for he had no near relatives and no friends at Court: he must not, therefore, rest idly on his oars, and must do something and be somebody; and he says that she succeeded in inspiring him with a great ambition to rise by his own efforts. Meanwhile he was carefully educated, first by a Jesuit at home—a Father Sanadon, the only member of the Order of whom he speaks with anything like respect. Then he was sent to the Academy at Rochefort, where he studied science and philosophy. But he tells us that he had no taste for metaphysics: what delighted him most were the chronicles and memoirs of his own country, and it was their perusal that first gave him the idea of writing his own. "My firm resolve to keep them entirely to myself appeared" (so he says) "to make up completely for the inconveniences that did not fail to occur to me."

CHAPTER III.

SAINT SIMON IN THE ARMY.

APPROACHING the mature age of seventeen, Saint Simon got tired of his books and lessons, and—excited by the example of his fellow-pupil, the young Duke of Chartres, then setting out for his first campaign—he induced his father to take him to Versailles and present him at Court. Louis received them both very graciously, and at once enrolled the young men in the regiment known as the " Grey Musketeers." The following year (1692), young Saint Simon set off to join the army in Flanders, with what would seem in these days an immense camp equipment for a cadet,—thirty-five horses or sumpter-mules, and two gentlemen in attendance, a tutor and a squire, charged by his mother with the special care of his person. Neither of these two guardians, however, seems to have been of much use to their young master. In the first action, the tutor lost his hat and wig, while his horse took the bit in his teeth and bolted with him into the enemy's lines; while the squire kept at a prudent distance from the firing, and only came up when it was all over, to congratulate people generally on the brilliant success of the day. " I was so surprised and indignant at his effrontery," says Saint Simon, "that I never answered him a word then, and have never spoken to him since."

This was one of the last campaigns in which Louis ever took the field in person. As usual, his Majesty was accompanied by an immense retinue,—marshals, princes of the blood, nobles with their equipages and attendants, and half the ladies of the Court, besides hosts of camp-followers, and endless trains of provisions, baggage-waggons, and artillery. A review was held in the plains near Mons, and 120,000 men were drawn up in two lines extending over eight miles of country. Then Namur, the strongest fortress in the Netherlands, was solemnly invested under the direction of Vauban, "the soul of sieges." Earthworks were thrown up, trenches were opened; parallels and escarpments were formed in a manner that would have delighted the heart of Corporal Trim; and all went well for the besiegers till the 8th of June, the day of Saint Medard, who answers to our Saint Swithin. On that day, unfortunately, a deluge of rain set in, and lasted without intermission for three weeks. The country became a quagmire; the roads were flooded, and the discomfort and difficulties caused were so great, that the soldiers, furious with the weather, broke and burnt every image of the unlucky Saint Medard that they could lay their hands on. Carts and waggons were useless for transport, owing to the mud, and everything required for the camp, from the gunpowder to the forage, had to be carried on the backs of mules and horses. The common troopers took their share of the fatigue-duty cheerfully enough; but when it came to the turn of the fine gentlemen of the king's guards to carry sacks of corn to Luxemburg's camp, they not only murmured loudly, but on one occasion threw down their sacks, and flatly refused to lift them on the horses.

"I arrived with my detachment of musketeers just as the guards made their refusal, and I loaded my sack before their eyes. Marin (the cavalry brigadier, and a lieutenant of the body-guards) saw me at the same moment, and, full of wrath at the refusal he had just met with, cried out—at the same time pointing me out, and calling my name—that, since *I* did not find this duty beneath me, the troopers and guardsmen need not feel it any dishonour or humiliation to follow my example. This reproof, joined to the severe air of Marin, had such an immediate effect, that instantly, without a word of reply, the guardsmen filled their sacks as quickly as possible."

Saint Simon's spirited conduct was repeated to Louis, and he received in consequence, as he tells us, many flattering marks of royal favour during this wearisome siege. Namur at last capitulated, and shortly afterwards the campaign itself came to an end; but the exultation of the French over the fall of the fortress was greatly damped by the news which had just come of the disastrous sea-fight off Cape La Hogue.

Saint Simon lost his father early in the following year (1693). "He died," he says, "almost before they had time to call out that he was ill,—there was no more oil in the lamp. I heard the sad news as I came back from the king's *coucher*. The night was given to the just sentiments of nature, and early the next morning I went to find Bontems" (the king's valet)—to secure his influence in procuring some of the offices held by his father.

The whole strength of the kingdom was now put forth, and five large armies took the field at once. Louis again assumed the command in person, and joined his forces with those of the Duke of Luxemburg on the Flemish frontier. The Prince of Orange found himself hemmed in by two armies, each of them superior to his own, and cut off from all supplies and reinforcements. As he said afterwards in a letter to a friend, he was caught in a trap, and nothing but a miracle could have saved him.

But suddenly, when Luxemburg was congratulating himself on this rare opportunity, Louis declared his intention of sending his own army off to the German frontier, and returning himself to Versailles. It was in vain that the Duke went on his knees and implored him with tears in his eyes to seize this chance of annihilating his enemy. Louis persisted in his resolution, and marched off the next day to join the ladies. His soldiers murmured openly; and the officers, high and low, could not conceal their disgust and disappointment at leaving such a promising campaign without drawing their swords.

"I chanced," says Saint Simon, "to be going alone on duty to M. de Luxemburg's headquarters, as I often used to do, merely to see what was going on, and what was likely to be the programme the next day. I was greatly surprised not to find a soul there, and to hear that every one was on the king's side of the camp. I was sitting there pensive and stock-still upon my horse, wondering what on earth this could mean, and debating whether I should return or push on to the king's army, when I saw the Prince de Conti coming from our camp, followed only by a page and a groom with a spare horse. 'What are you doing there?' he cried out as he joined me, laughing at my surprise; and he explained that he was just going to wish the king good-bye, and that I had better go with him to do the same. 'What do you mean by wishing good-bye?' I asked. Then he ordered his page and his groom to follow him at a little distance, and asked me to tell my lackey to do the same. And then he told me all about the retreat of the king, dying with laughter, and made tremendous fun of it all—for he completely trusted me, in spite of my youth. I listened with all my ears, and my inexpressible astonishment stopped my asking any questions. Chatting together in this manner, we met all the world on their way back, and we joined them."

The next day Louis set off for Namur, where the ladies were waiting for him, and from Namur returned to Versailles. Left to himself, Luxemburg at once marched after the Prince of Orange, and found him encamped in a strong position near Neerwinden.

Saint Simon gives us a graphic, though confused, account of this battle—next to Malplaquet and Waterloo, the bloodiest ever fought in that part of Europe. It was the only action he was ever engaged in, and he tells us with pardonable vanity how his own regiment charged five times; how his colonel and brigadier were killed; and how a gold button was shot away from his own doublet. He has left us a description of the hero of the day—the Duke of Luxemburg—who was, if Marlborough be excepted, the greatest captain of the century:—

"Nothing could be more exact than the *coup d'œil* of M. de Luxemburg; nothing could be more brilliant, more carefully planned, more far-sighted than he showed himself in presence of the enemy, or on a day of battle, coupled with an audacity, a playfulness, and a *sang froid* that allowed him to see everything, and to foresee everything in the midst of the hottest fire, and of the most imminent danger. It was there that he was really great. For the rest he was idleness itself. He rarely walked, unless there was some great necessity; gambling, conversation with his intimate friends, and every evening a supper with a very small number (nearly always the same); and if he was encamped near any town, care was taken that the fair sex should be agreeably mingled with the other guests. At such times Luxemburg was inaccessible to all the world, and if any emergency occurred, it was Puységur (the second in command) who gave the orders. Such was the life of this great general when with the army, and such it was also at Paris, when the Court and the great world occupied his days and pleasure his evenings."

Saint Simon occupied the interval between his two campaigns characteristically enough—in bringing a lawsuit against the great Marshal whom he has just described. It is quite clear that the details of this question of precedence, which would in modern days have been decided by the Heralds' College or by the Committee of Privileges in half an hour, have a far greater interest and importance in his eye than all the battles ever fought. Luxemburg had claimed the dormant title of the Duke of Piney—a title dating from 1581—which, if proved, would give him precedence over all the dukes except one on the roll of peers. To substantiate this claim, he had (according to Saint Simon) ferreted out the daughter and heiress of the last Duke of Piney by his *second* wife, and married her, although she was "hideously ugly, like some frightfully fat fishwoman in her cask;" and then he had bribed the real heirs (the children of the *first* wife)—an imbecile priest and his sister who had taken the veil—to waive their claims to the title and estates. Lastly, he had got himself created Duke of Piney by new letters-patent, dating from 1662

All this was monstrous, according to Saint Simon. The ancient title was virtually extinct, or, if not extinct, should have descended to the imbecile priest shut up in St Lazare. And so he induced his brother peers to enter on their hopeless crusade against Luxemburg's claim; but, as he confesses himself, everything was against them from the first. Just then Luxemburg was the hero of the hour, fresh from a victorious campaign, the friend of royalty, and popular with all men of all classes —" in a word, the ladies, the rising generation, all the fashion of Court and town, were for him; and no one on our side was strong enough to counterbalance the weight of these grandees, or even to make any head against their influence; and if one adds to this the pains he took beforehand to cultivate the goodwill of the chief men both in Parliament and the Chamber of Peers by means of parents, friends, mistresses, confessors, valets, promises, services, it will be clear that with a First President like Harlay at the head of this faction, we had a business on hand incomparably too strong for us."

The case was argued and reargued before the Parliament, and after various delays and postponements, during which Luxemburg himself died, and his son became the defendant, judgment was at last given in favour of the title dating from 1662, while the decision as to Luxemburg's claim to the title of 1581 was indefinitely postponed. Thus things were left pretty much as they were before.

Saint Simon's indignation at this verdict is almost ludicrous. By his account, the peers would have won their suit, in spite of the formidable odds against them, had it not been for the villany of Harlay, the First

President (or, as we might say, the Lord Chancellor), who had sold his influence to the opposite party; and then, by way of revenge, he paints Harlay's character for us in the blackest colours. After doing unwilling justice to the President's knowledge of the law and his profound and varied learning, he speaks of his "pharisaical austerity" and his craft as a politician, and then he concludes—

"He was destitute of real honour, secretly depraved in morals, with only a show of honesty, without even humanity,—in a word, a perfect hypocrite; without a faith, without a law, without a God, and without a soul; a cruel husband, a barbarous father, a tyrannical brother; no one's friend but his own; wicked by nature; taking delight in insulting, outraging, and crushing (others), and having never, during all his life, missed a chance of doing so.[1]

---

[1] Saint Simon says, "It is a pity some one has not made a *Harleiana* of all his sayings, which would show the character of this cynic, and would be amusing at the same time." He has done his best to supply this want himself; and of the many stories he tells us of the caustic humour of the First President, the following is too good to be omitted. "The Duchess of La Ferté went to him [Harlay] to ask an audience, and, like every one else, had a taste of his temper. As she was leaving, she complained to her man of business, and called the First President 'an old baboon.' He was following her all the while, but did not say a word. At last she saw him behind her, but hoped that he had not overheard, and, without giving any sign of having done so, he put her in her carriage.

"Shortly afterwards her suit came on (before Harlay), and she unexpectedly gained her cause. Off she ran to the First President's house, and made him all kinds of acknowledgments. He—all humble and modest—made her a deep reverence, and then looking her straight in the face,—'Madame,' said he in a loud voice before everybody, 'I am very glad that an old baboon (*un vieux singe*) has been able to give some pleasure to an old she-monkey (*une veille guenon*).' And then, in his humblest manner, without saying another word, he gave her his hand to conduct her to her carriage. The Duchess would have liked to have killed him or died herself."

"In appearance he was a small man, wiry and vigorous; with a lozenge-shaped face, a long aquiline nose, fine-speaking, piercing eyes that only looked at you askance, but which, if fixed on a client or a magistrate, were like to make him sink into the ground. He wore a robe that was somewhat short, collar and wristbands plaited like those of a priest's, a brown wig mixed with white, well stuffed but short, with a great cap above it. He stooped, and walked a little bent, with a studied air more humble than modest, and continually scraped along the walls to make people give way to him with greater noise; and at Versailles made his way with respectful, and, as it were, shamefaced bows to the right and left."

About this time Saint Simon married a daughter of the Marshal de Lorges, and to her excellent qualities of head as well as heart he owed, he says, the chief happiness of his life. He describes her as being "fair, with a perfect complexion and figure, and with a bearing at once extremely noble and modest, and with a something I know not what of majesty, tempered with an air of virtue and natural sweetness."[1] The wedding was celebrated in the Church of St Roch, and the curious may still see in the parish register the signatures of the bride and bridegroom,—Saint Simon's in a bold, large hand, very unlike his usual small, neat writing; and the bride's in a school-girl's copperplate style. There was a grand banquet after the ceremony, a *levée* the next morning, and in the evening they were invited to

[1] The 'Mercurie Galant'—the 'Morning Post' of that day—does justice to the bride's personal appearance, and adds that she had "a beauty of soul, such as a person of quality ought to have, that will make her a fitting match for her husband the duke—one of the wisest and most accomplished seigneurs of the Court." It is not often that Saint Simon gets such high compliments from contemporary journals.

supper at Versailles, where Louis received the young duchess in his most gracious and stately manner.

For obvious reasons Saint Simon did not choose to serve again under Luxemburg. Accordingly he changed his regiment and joined the army of the Rhine under his father-in-law, the Marshal de Lorges. But he tells us very little about this campaign, beyond the Marshal's dangerous illness, when Saint Simon saved the old man's life by administering "a hundred and thirty English drops," which, we are told, had "an astonishing effect." In Flanders, he says that a large part of the Prince of Orange's army under Vaudemont might have been easily surrounded and cut off, had it not been for the cowardice of the Duke of Maine, the king's favourite son. Message after message was sent him from headquarters, urging him to attack the enemy; but he "stammered out excuses," and allowed Vaudemont's force to make good their retreat.[1] "All our army were in despair," Saint Simon adds, "and both officers and men made no scruple of expressing their indignation and contempt."

It was some time before the king heard of his son's poltroonery, for Villeroy was far too good a courtier to tell all he knew in his despatches, and his subordinates held their tongues. At last Louis suspected something of the real state of the case, and cross-questioned Lavienne, one

---

[1] Here, again, we are told that Saint Simon has been led away by his hatred of "the Bastard." Two eyewitnesses of what occurred—Berwick and Saint Hilaire—give an entirely different version of the story, and attribute the delay in the attack to Marshal Villeroy, and not to the Duke of Maine—(see Chéruel, p. 625). Macaulay accepts Saint Simon's account (as he usually does) without scruple or question—(History, iv. 587).

of his valets, who reluctantly told him the whole story. Louis's anger and mortification were extreme.

"This prince, outwardly so calm and such a master of his slightest movements, even when events touched him most nearly, succumbed on this single occasion. As he was leaving the table at Marly with all the ladies, and in the presence of all the courtiers, he saw a servant who, while clearing away the dessert, put a biscuit in his pocket. In an instant the king forgets all his dignity, and with a cane in his hand which they had just brought him with his hat, he rushes upon the valet, who was not in the least expecting such an attack, strikes him, abuses him, and breaks the cane upon his shoulders (as a matter of fact it was only of rosewood, and did not resist in the least). And then, with the handle in his hand, and with the air of a man who cannot contain himself, and all the time abusing this valet, who was by this time a long way off, he crossed the smaller *salon* and an antechamber, and entered Madame de Maintenon's room, where he remained nearly an hour, as he often did at Marly after dinner. As he was leaving her room to pass to his own, he saw Père la Chaise, and as soon as he perceived him among the crowd of courtiers—'My father,' he said in a loud voice, 'I have just beaten a rascal and have broken my cane on his back, but I do not believe that I have offended God'—and then he told the story of the pretended offence. All who were present trembled still more at what they had just seen and heard."

After the Peace of Ryswick, Saint Simon's own regiment was disbanded with many others; and about the same time thirty-eight brigadiers of cavalry were gazetted at once, but he looked in vain for his own name among the list. Five younger officers, who had probably paid a large sum for their promotion, were placed over his head, and in disgust he threw up his commission—acting, he tells us, by the advice of some of his older friends. He wrote a civil letter to the king, making ill-health the excuse for having left the service. But Louis was annoyed, as he always was when any officer sent in his resignation. "See, Monsieur, here is another man who is leaving us," he remarked to the Secretary of War, on reading Saint Simon's letter; and it was long, we are told, before he forgot or forgave what he regarded as a personal slight. For years Saint Simon received no invitations to Marly—and there was no surer sign of royal disfavour.

CHAPTER IV.

VERSAILLES.

SAINT SIMON does unwilling justice—if indeed he can be said to do justice at all—to Louis XIV.'s character. He tells us that "he had received from God ability enough to be a good king, and possibly a sufficiently great king,"[1] but that he had been corrupted by "the mortal poison of flattery;" that he was supremely vain and selfish; that his education had been neglected; that history, law, and science were sealed books to him; and that he disliked and discouraged anything like superior talent in others.

Socially (even by Saint Simon's account), Louis was the first gentleman of his day—a king among men. Every accomplishment seemed to come naturally to him. He was a good dancer, a skilful tennis-player, a bold rider, and a first-rate marksman.

"His figure, his carriage, the grace, the beauty, and the grand bearing which exceeded the beauty, even to the sound of his voice and mode of speaking, and the natural and majestic grace of his whole person, made him as remarkable, even up to the day of his death, as the queen bee of the hive

---

[1] Mazarin, who knew Louis XIV. better than Saint Simon did, declared that "he had stuff enough in him to make four kings and an honest man."

(*le roi des abeilles*); and if he had only been born an ordinary person, he would have equally had the talent for *fêtes*, for pleasures, for gallantry, and for the distractions of love.

"Never did any one give with a better grace, and thereby enhance so largely the value of his gifts. Never did any one give such distinction to his words, his smiles—nay, to his very looks. He made everything precious by making it choice and majestic, and to this the rarity and brevity of his words added not a little. If he addressed any one,—a question it might be, or some commonplace remark,—all the bystanders noticed the favoured individual: it was an honour about which one talked, and which always became a sort of consideration. It was the same with all his attentions and distinctions, and with the preferences so exactly proportioned to each person's merits. Never did he so far forget himself as to say anything disobliging of anybody; and if he had to find fault, to reprimand, or to correct (which was seldom the case), it was always with an air of kindness, rarely with harshness or severity, and never with anger."

Louis wished that Versailles should absorb the nobility of France. All the great nobles held offices in the household, which made their constant presence necessary; and a town had grown up around the palace, where each of them had his separate establishment. To such men the country was regarded as a desert, to which no one would be banished if he could help it. Thus, while between Paris and Versailles there was an endless stream of coaches and carriages passing and repassing, along the highroad between Paris and Orleans the traveller would meet nothing but a few peasants' carts, some soldiers on the march, or a messenger posting towards the frontier. "All France was there," is a common expression of Saint Simon's, in referring to some Court ceremonial; and assuredly all the life and splendour of the time was to be found at Versailles. At every *levée* the king looked right and left of him, with a glance that nothing could escape, and showed marked disapprobation of those who did not present themselves regularly. If a favour was asked for any of these absentees,—"Who is he?" was the reply. "I don't know him. He is a man I never see." His memory in these cases was never at fault. He would recognise, says Saint Simon, some ordinary person whom he had perhaps only seen once, after the lapse of twenty years, and would not only remember his face, but the circumstances of their last interview.

Saint Simon could no more have lived away from Versailles than a man in modern society could be away from London in the season; and though, as has been said, he had too much temper, and too much honour, to play the courtier himself,[1] Court life had special and irresistible attractions for him. Versailles was, so to speak, his hunting-ground,—the arena where he watched with insatiable curiosity the great human drama with all its varying scenes — the plots and counterplots — the intrigues and ambitions—the rise and fall of courtier after courtier—the passions and vanities of this little world, and all its medley of tragedy and farce. The study of character seems to have had an ever-increasing fascination for him, and to have consoled him in a measure for his own isolation among the brilliant throng of nobles and princes, most of whom he so cordially hated and despised. These "insects of the Court," as he disdain-

---

[1] It was of Antin that the Regent Orleans said, "Voila comme un vrai courtier devoit être—sans humeur et sans honneur." If we reverse the proposition, it will exactly apply to Saint Simon.

fully terms them, had a scientific value in his eyes, for they could be analysed and dissected by the man who could read their hearts; their vices and their virtues could be weighed in the balance; and every word and gesture could be scrutinised and referred to its originating motive. Accordingly it was in the moments of some supreme agony or crisis, when the most practised actor was forced to drop his mask for the time being and show himself for once in his real character, that Saint Simon's powers of observation were excited to their keenest point, and he then became all eyes and ears to mark and note the scene as it passed before him.

"It must be confessed," he says, "that for him who knows the Court to its inmost corners, the first sight of rare spectacles of this kind,[1] so interesting in so many different points of view, gives an extreme satisfaction. Each face recalls to you the cares, the intrigues, the intense labour employed in the advancement and formation of fortunes by the aid of cabals; the skill used to hold one's own ground and get rid of others; the means of all kinds employed to that end; the intimacies more or less advanced; the estrangements, the coldnesses, the hatreds, the ill turns, the intrigues, the overtures, the diplomacy, the meanness, the baseness of each; the disconcertment of some when half-way on their road, or in the midst, or at the height of their expectations; . . . all this medley of living objects and of such important details give to him who knows how to receive it a pleasure which, hollow as it may seem, is one of the greatest that you can enjoy at Court."

It may perhaps help to explain the ideas and associations which Saint Simon attaches to this hateful word "courtier," if we take the character selected by himself,

[1] He is speaking of the famous scene at Versailles after Monseigneur's death—see v. 152.

and by Sainte Beuve after him, as their type of the courtier *par excellence*. This was Antin, the only legitimate son of Madame de Montespan, and the half-brother of the Dukes of Maine and Toulouse. It is clear, even by Saint Simon's account, that Antin had been singularly gifted with almost every mental and bodily accomplishment that a man can need to hold his own in society,—a fine presence, charming manners, talent, learning, knowledge of the world, powers of conversation, wit and humour; and, above all, he had what is perhaps the rarest of all social virtues—"never did he chance to speak ill of any one." But Saint Simon would have us believe that Antin, with all his fascinating qualities, was "an impudent Gascon,"—base, false, and avaricious—a gambler, a cheat, and, above all, a coward. He had turned his back in the day of battle, and had accepted the grossest insults without venturing to retaliate, and that at a time when courage was the first instinct of a nobleman, and when cowardice was a brand on a man's character that nothing could efface. "It was looked upon as disgraceful," says Saint Simon, "to insult Antin,"—just as it would be now to strike a woman.

Still, in spite of his shortcomings, there can be no doubt that Antin was the most popular man of the day. He had contrived to make himself so useful and agreeable to all parties at Court that he was equally at home both at Meudon and Versailles. The king liked his lively conversation and his knowledge of life and character; and Monseigneur always found him good company, and ready to gamble from night till morning. As an instance of the trouble he took to ingratiate himself with Madame de Maintenon, Saint Simon tells us that, when she visited him at Petit Bourg, she found her boudoir arranged as an exact duplicate of her own room at Versailles—the same decorations, the same pictures, the same flowers, and even the same books, lying open in the same place. But even this delicate attention did not mollify the great lady, for she went out of her way to sneer at his complaisance before she left Petit Bourg. Louis was more easily pleased, and admired all he saw.

"Everything was highly approved of, except an avenue of chestnut-trees, which, though they looked marvellously well from the gardens, blocked up the view from the window of the king's room. Antin said not a word; but when the king awoke the next morning, and looked out of his window, he saw the most charming view in the world, and no avenue in sight, and no trace of there having been one in the place where he had seen it the night before. Nor were there any traces of workmen nor of removal along the whole length of the line, nor in any part of the gardens near it. It was as if the avenue had never existed. No one had heard any noise or disturbance in the night; the trees had disappeared, and the earth was so completely levelled that it seemed as if the transformation must have been produced by the wand of some beneficent fairy in this enchanted castle."

We have selected Antin as being the type of his class, but Saint Simon would tell us that there were a thousand like him, or even worse than him, incessantly hanging about the Court; and it was the sight of such men daily receiving honours and rewards, and all the good things of this life, that rankled so deeply in his mind. Added to this was the sense of his own unrequited merits, and of his powerlessness to remedy the evil and injustice of the case. These feelings explain, and in some degree excuse, the bitter and uncharitable tone of many of his portraits. Christian as he was, he could not be at charity with men whom he believed to be hypocrites and rascals. "One is charmed," he says, "with true and honest men; one is irritated against the scoundrels who swarm at Court, still more against those who have done us an injury. The Stoic is a fine and noble chimera. I don't pique myself on impartiality, and I should vainly try to do so." In fact, it was a point of conscience with him, if he described such men as Antin at all, to describe them as he saw them, not as they appeared to their ignorant and foolish admirers,—to strip off the mask that concealed their features, and lay bare every secret corner of their hearts; to paint them in their true colours, not to gloss over their foibles and their vices; to paint them (if we may borrow Macaulay's illustration), as Lely painted Cromwell, with all his warts and wrinkles, or as Rembrandt painted his burgomaster, with every line and shadow traced by time upon his face,—and not to give us a gallery of portraits insipid and unreal, and unlike the actual men.

There is no doubt that, in many instances, Saint Simon has over-coloured these portraits: indeed we may trust, for the credit of humanity, that the courtiers of his day were not quite the angels of darkness that he represents them, and that there was more honour and honesty to be found among them than he is willing to allow. But just as Carlyle discovered "shams" in almost every phase of modern life, and as Thackeray invented "snobs" to fill up his forty chapters, — so Saint Simon has made the most of his grand topic for reproof and scorn and denunciation, and has selected "the courtier" as his text for a hundred sermons.

There are two famous chapters in La Bruyère, where he describes the Court and fashion of the day much in the same bitter and satirical spirit. Like our writer, La Bruyère maintains that the courtier's name is legion —an inexhaustible species, embracing all kinds and degrees of gilded servitude, from "the satellites of Jupiter," the most favoured personal friends of royalty, to the humbler but not less ambitious parasites, who hang about the anterooms and galleries on the chance of a passing look or smile from their patrons.

In fact, the courtier's life at Versailles was a faint reflection of the king's. From the moment that he opened his eyes in the morning till he closed them at night, Louis was always (so to speak) on parade—in full-dress order. He could not even take his medicine or eat his broth if he was ill, without an usher first summoning the *grande entrée;* and every detail of his ordinary life was regulated, as Saint Simon tells us, by the most tedious etiquette. Even his *levée* was a long and stately ceremony —a kind of drama in five acts; and his toilet took place in the presence of a large audience, when one favoured courtier would hold the candlestick, another would take the towel after his Majesty had washed his hands, while to hand the shirt was a privilege reserved for a prince of the blood-royal. Then came private audiences; and shortly afterwards the captain of the guard threw open the folding doors of the cabinet, and Louis walked along the gallery that led to the chapel, bowing right and left to the line of courtiers as he passed them.

Mass was then celebrated, and the courtiers gazed with all their eyes on the king as he remained on his knees before the altar. "One cannot help seeing a sort of subordination in their worship," says La Bruyère, "for the people seem to adore the prince, and the prince to adore God."

When Mass was over the king returned to his private room, and his Ministers followed him with their portfolios; and on four mornings of the week he held a cabinet council—latterly always in Madame de Maintenon's room. Dinner was served at one o'clock. Except when he was with the army, no man under the rank of a prince of the blood ever dined with the king: the courtiers remained standing behind his chair; and even his brother, "Monsieur," was only occasionally honoured with a seat at the same table. The king had a royal appetite, and his dinner always consisted of several rich soups and four or five courses of meat, concluding with dessert, ices, and sweetmeats.[1] "If he made me eat half as much as he eats himself, I should not be long alive," wrote Madame de Maintenon in 1713.

When dinner was over, the king entered his cabinet again, fed his dogs, changed his dress (again in public), and then went down by the private stairs to the marble court, where his coach was waiting. Sometimes, instead of driving, he would go out hunting, though he gave this up latterly, or shoot in the park, or drive a four-in-hand through the forest of Fontainebleau; and we are told that no professional coachman ever handled the reins with such skill and grace. As he grew older, his exercise

---

[1] "I have often," writes Madame de Bavière, "seen the king eat four plates of different soups, a whole pheasant, a partridge, a large plate of salad, two good slices of ham, a plate of pastry, and then be helped more than once to fruit and sweetmeats."

generally took the form of a promenade round the gardens, where he would feed the carp, watch the fountains playing, and chat with his gardener, Le Nôtre; and often for four or five hours his courtiers had to follow his Majesty in all weathers up and down the long terraces, with their heads only sheltered by their periwigs; but, as the Abbé de Polignac once said, when Louis hoped that his purple dress would not be spoiled by a sudden shower—"It is nothing, Sire; the rain of Marly never wets one." It was only at Marly that the king ever gave the welcome order, "Your hats, gentlemen," when they all covered.

Sometimes, instead of the stately promenade, there would be a picnic (*fête champêtre*), or a garden-party, when tents were pitched under the trees of Saint Germains, or in one of the long alleys at Fontainebleau; or the courtiers rowed in gondolas along the broad canal at Versailles, and did not return till after sunset.

At Marly the ladies of the Court always had supper at the royal table; but here again everything was regulated by the strictest etiquette. One evening Madame de Torcy (the Minister's wife) happened to come in late, and took a seat that was vacant above the Duchess de Duvas. Louis almost petrified her with a look of anger and astonishment, and complained to Madame de Maintenon afterwards that he had never seen such "incredible insolence on the part of a little *bourgeoise*." He constantly reverted to the subject, and did not—so Saint Simon says—recover his equanimity for three whole days.

After supper the long gallery and the whole of that magnificent suite of rooms were lighted up with countless chandeliers, and the splendour of the scene can only be faintly realised from the pictures left to us of the time—the laced ruffles, the silken coats, and gold embroidery worn by the courtiers, and the ladies' dresses sparkling (as a writer describes them) like a rich espalier of pearls, gold, jewels, flowers, and fruits. Sometimes there would be a fancy ball or a masquerade, when the maids of honour represented the seasons of the year, or some scene from mythology; or a fair, where the ladies kept stalls and sold curiosities from China and Japan; or a lottery, where Louis distributed jewels and trinkets to the winners of lucky numbers. In 1700 there was a ball every night for three weeks; and Saint Simon says, "One did not leave till eight o'clock in the morning. I was heartily glad when Lent came, and remained almost dead with fatigue for two or three days, and Madame de Saint Simon could hardly get over Shrove-Tuesday."

As to the games of chance played on ordinary evenings, their names are as numerous as those played by Gargantua himself. Lansquenet, piquet, ombre, brelan, basset, are a few out of the many mentioned; and in Saint Simon's own country-house (as we learn by the inventory of the furniture) there were six tables devoted to different games in one room. Some cool-headed players like Dangeau, who combined luck with skill, would win a hundred thousand francs at basset in ten days. Others, like Antin, were supposed to aid fortune by occasional cheating.

"'Pray, Monseigneur,' asked the king one day of his son, 'is it true that while you were playing and gaining heavily, you gave your hat to Antin to hold while you threw your winnings into it, and that as you turned your head by chance, you surprised Antin pocketing the money?' Monseigneur said nothing in reply, but only looked at the king and bowed his head to signify that it was even as he had said. 'I understand you, Monseigneur,' said the king. 'I ask nothing more about it.' And thereupon they separated."[1]

Certainly some of the stories told us by Saint Simon reveal an undercurrent of coarseness and ill-breeding, which we should hardly have suspected to have lain hid under the solemn formalities of the most stately Court in history. We hear of the princesses borrowing pipes and tobacco from the Swiss guards, and holding a sort of orgie when the king had retired for the night, or letting off crackers under Monsieur's windows at midnight, to his great indignation; we hear of one great lady calling another a wine-sack, and the other replying that it was better to be a wine-sack than a rag-sack; we hear of the Duchess of Berry being carried to bed drunk after a supper-party, and of the "Grand Squire" grossly insulting a Grand Duchess at Monseigneur's card-table.

Human nature needs some relief from perpetual constraint, and as the gravest kings had their jesters to amuse their idle moments, so at Versailles there were professed buffoons and butts for ridicule, ready-made to endure every sort of insult and practical joke, without venturing on resistance or retaliation. A creature of this kind was the Princess d'Harcourt—"a sort of personage," says Saint Simon, "whom it is a good thing to make known, in order to know more thoroughly a

[1] Saint Simon's authority for this story is the first squire, who told it to him "with an air of ravishment," having heard it himself from one of the valets.

Court which did not scruple to receive such beings;" and then he describes her: "Tall, fat, the colour of milk-porridge, with thick ugly lips, and hair like tow . . . Dirty and sluttish, always intriguing, pretending, attempting, always quarrelling, . . . she was a white fury—nay more, she was a Harpy, for she had all the effrontery, the wickedness, the deceit and violence of one, as well as its avarice and greediness."

Although nominally a *dévote* of Madame de Maintenon's type, this princess cheated at cards in the most barefaced manner, and stormed and screamed if detected. She flew into fits of blind passion on the smallest provocation, and abused and beat her servants, until one stalwart chambermaid retaliated, locked the door, and then belaboured her mistress with a broom-handle till she howled for mercy. One cold winter's night, some of the more mischievous courtiers, headed by Saint Simon's model prince, the Duke of Burgundy, got into her room and pelted her with snowballs.

"This filthy creature in her bed, roused from sleep with a start, bruised and drenched with the snow all over her ears and head, dishevelled, screaming at the top of her voice, and wriggling like an eel, without knowing where to hide herself, was a sight that diverted them all for more than half an hour; so that the nymph floated in her bed, while the water, trickling from it on all sides, flooded the whole room. It was enough to make one burst with laughter. The next day she sulked and was laughed at more than ever."

It is hardly credible that this brutality should have occurred at Versailles; yet Saint Simon describes the scene as if he had himself taken part in it. To half-drown a defenceless woman with snow on a winter's night is a piece of malicious horseplay, that might have come naturally from Panurge or Friar John, but seems strangely out of place in a Court celebrated for the perfection of fine manners, where the king would gravely take his hat off to the humblest chambermaid, and in an age when vice itself was supposed to have " lost half its evil by losing all its grossness."

"Would to God," says Saint Simon, "that Madame de Maintenon had only women like Madame de Dangeau about her!" He describes most of her friends and favourites as having no redeeming qualities except extreme servility and *dévotion à l'outrance.* For instance, there was the family of Heudicourt, all of whom seemed to have been well received at Court. Of the mother, Saint Simon says no one could possibly have been "more gratuitously, more continuously, more desperately wicked." Her husband was "an old rascal, extremely debauched, and the son was a species of satyr as wicked as, and even uglier than, the father; a great drunkard, yet irresistible with the ladies, who worshipped him, and always spoke of him as 'the good little fellow.'"

Another charming creature, who " was at all the Marlys, although the horror of all the world," was the Princess de Montauban, who we are told was "humpbacked, all on one side, extremely ugly, and covered with white paint, rouge, and blue lines to mark the veins, tricked out with patches, ornaments, and trinkets, which she kept on till more than eighty, when she died. Nothing was so shameless, so dissolute, so greedy, so strangely wicked as this sort of monster, although she had plenty of talent of the worst kind, and could often make herself agreeable when it pleased her."

Space forbids our dwelling further on these pictures of the ladies of the Court—still less can we follow Saint Simon through those "laughable adventures," those "ridiculous situations," those "pleasant anecdotes," that so often form the headings of his chapters. Those who make the search for themselves will be well repaid for their trouble. Nothing in Molière's comedies is more ludicrous than some of these scenes from Court life: Madame de Rupelmonde playing cards in the crowded drawing-room at Marly, and gravely ordered to go to bed by the Swiss groom of the chambers; the old Madame de St Herem, who was so afraid of thunder that she used to get under her bed and make all her servants get on top of it, piled one above the other, and who had love made to her in rather too demonstrative a fashion by an escaped lunatic ("she was hideous at eighteen, and was then eighty," says Saint Simon, parenthetically); the romantic love-story of La Coetlogon; the troubles of La Meilleraye, whose husband, St Ruth, kept her in order with a cudgel; the eccentricities of Lauzun; the pranks of Coislin and Courcillon,—all these are some of the "bagatelles" which Saint Simon apologises for recounting, but which, as he justly says, give life and reality to his picture of the times.

CHAPTER V.

PRINCES AND PRINCESSES.

No spot of country is at once so interesting and so melancholy as the valley of the Seine round Paris. Each hill and village, as we see them from the railroad, recalls its memories of the past; each palace and chateau are associated with the reign of the great king; and wherever we tread in this region, "a history is beneath our feet." Versailles in its lonely magnificence; the deserted Trianons; the valley of Port Royal, as desolate as Glencoe itself; the ruined walls of Saint Cyr; Marly, almost buried in the forest, where only a few green mounds mark the site of Louis's favourite retreat; Saint Cloud, once "the home of all delights," now a heap of blackened ruins; Saint Germains, the most picturesque of all, with the long terrace along which James II. walked, now disfigured by a hotel, and the galleries where Henry IV. held his Court, vulgarised by a museum; the vast palace of the Condés at Chantilly gone for ever, and their hunting-lodge only left to its present owner; Sceaux, so famous for its *fêtes* and brilliant society, demolished to make room for a school of agriculture,—turn where we will, there is the same story of neglect, or desecration, or destruction.

But, in Saint Simon's time, each of these palaces was Versailles on a smaller scale. Le Nôtre had planned the park, and laid out the gardens; Mansard had designed the rooms; Le Brun had painted the ceilings; a royal prince held his Court there, with his own set of courtiers, his parasites, his lackeys, his troops of servants and retainers. There was an endless stream of visitors, who passed much as they do now from one country-house to another,—great hunting-parties, balls and masquerades, and gambling protracted to the small hours of the morning. Saint Cloud seems to have been the most popular of all these abodes of royalty. It served as a half-way house between Paris and Versailles, and was constantly filled with nobles going to or coming from the Court. "The pleasures of every kind of game, the singular beauty of the place itself, with a thousand carriages standing ready for the legions of sightseers, the music, the good cheer—all this," says Saint Simon, "made of it a palace of delights."

The master of Saint Cloud was Monsieur, the king's brother, the noisiest and liveliest of the Bourbons—short, corpulent, without natural dignity, always steeped in perfumes and bedizened with jewellery, a great talker, and a great glutton,—affable and polite, and good-natured to excess. But, excepting that he had courage and a certain knowledge of the world, he was absolutely good for nothing,—a weak, suspicious, meddlesome busybody.

Monsieur's first wife was Henrietta of England, a charming and accomplished princess, but she had died suddenly in 1670. Then he had married the daughter of the Elector Palatine, generally known as "Madame de Bavière," who was as masculine in her habits as her husband was effeminate. She was German at heart, and never really domesticated herself in her French home. All her affections turned to her beloved Heidelberg, where she would rather (she says) have a good plate of sourkrout and smoked sausages than all the delicacies you could offer her. While Monsieur was hunting, or entertaining his friends at Saint Cloud, Madame was taking long solitary walks, or writing interminable letters in a little back room with German paladins depicted on the tapestry, or talking with her little German maid Bessola.

Saint Simon always speaks respectfully of Madame. Although she had "the figure and the roughness of a Swiss guard," she was true and honest—sincere both in her likes and dislikes—and these were rare qualities at Versailles. Moreover, she shared his abhorrence of Madame de Maintenon. "All the evil," she says, "that has yet been written of this diabolical woman, still falls short of the actual truth." She especially disliked to see the young princesses waiting upon the great lady, handing her the dishes and changing the plates. Madame looked on in silent indignation, and when asked to help them—"*I* have not been brought up to such mean services," she answered, "and am too old to give myself up to such child's play."

Madame's pride suffered a severe blow in 1692. The king had determined that her son, then the Duke de Chartres and afterwards 'the Regent Orleans, should marry Mademoiselle de Blois—one of his illegitimate daughters. Naturally enough, Madame's strict notions of propriety were outraged by the mere thought of such a *mésalliance*, but she could not help herself.

Louis had set his heart on the marriage; neither her husband nor her son dared to say a word against it; and Madame had to give her consent,—which she gave, says Saint Simon, "with tears in her eyes and fury in her heart." The same evening—

"I found all the world talking in little groups, and great astonishment depicted on every face. Madame kept walking up and down the gallery with her favourite maid of honour—striding along with great steps, her handkerchief in her hand, talking and gesticulating in a loud tone, and acting admirably the part of Ceres furiously searching for her daughter Proserpine, and demanding her back from Jupiter. Every one left the ground clear for her, and only passed through the gallery on their way to the drawing-room. Monseigneur and Monsieur had sat down to lansquenet; and never was anything so shamefaced and utterly disconcerted as Monsieur's countenance and whole appearance. His son (the Duke of Chartres) seemed in despair, and the bride-elect in the greatest sorrow and embarrassment.

. . . .

"At supper the king showed his usual ease of manner. Madame's eyes were full of tears, which fell from time to time, though she dried them now and then, as she looked round at every face as if to see what they thought of it all. Her son also had his eyes very red, and neither of them could eat anything. I noticed that the king offered Madame nearly all the dishes in front of him, and that she refused them all with a rudeness which did not in the least diminish his air of respect and politeness. It was also much remarked that after leaving the table, and when the circle round his Majesty was dispersing, the king made a very marked and low reverence to Madame, during which she performed such a complete pirouette that the king, as he raised his head, found nothing but her back towards him, only removed a step nearer the door.

. . . .

"The next morning Madame was at the *levée*, and her son approached her, as he did every day, to kiss her hand. But just then Madame gave him such a sounding box on the ear, that it was heard some paces off, and, delivered as it was in the presence of the whole Court, covered the unfortunate prince with confusion, and excited prodigious astonishment in the crowd of lookers-on, of whom I was one."

Monsieur soon disappears from the Memoirs. His life of gluttony and dissipation had ruined his health; and one morning his confessor—"good little Father Trévoux"—told him plainly that *he* was not going to be damned on Monsieur's account; that he must change his habits and take care of himself; that he was old, used-up, fat, short-necked, and to all appearances would die of apoplexy, and that very soon. These were terrible words (says Saint Simon) to a prince, "the most voluptuous and most attached to life that has ever been known;" and Monsieur said his prayers more frequently, grew *triste*, and talked less than usual—"that is to say, only about as much as three or four women."

Shortly afterwards there was a scene between him and the king at Marly, in which both lost their tempers, and Monsieur came out from the interview with his face so flushed and inflamed with passion, that some of the ladies suggested he should be bled at once—"but more for the sake of saying something than anything else." Unfortunately, however, his surgeon was old and not skilful with the lancet,—"he had missed fire before." Monsieur did not wish to be bled by him, and, in order not to vex him, would not be bled by any one else. The consequence was that he died of apoplexy the same evening. There was great consternation both at Marly and Saint Cloud, and the usual confusion followed in the household—the women especially, "who had lost their amusement and consideration, running hither and thither, and shrieking with dishevelled hair like so many Bacchantes." The king wept a good deal. Madame shut herself up in her room, and, "in the midst of her grief, kept calling out 'No convent! Let no one speak of a convent! I will have nothing to do with a convent!' This excellent princess had not lost her reason, for she knew by the terms of her marriage settlement that when she became a widow, she might choose between a chateau and a convent." As a matter of fact she retired to neither one nor the other, but still lived on at Saint Cloud.

At Chantilly was the palace of the Condés, and here lived Henri de Bourbon, generally known as "M. le Prince," the son of the great soldier of the Fronde. Saint Simon gives him a terribly bad character; all the nobler qualities of the "Grand Condé" seemed to have been distorted and perverted in his successor,— "an unnatural son, a cruel father, a terrible husband, a detestable master, a dangerous neighbour; without friendship and without friends, and incapable of having any."

His unfortunate wife suffered terribly from his fits of passion; and although she was herself "disgustingly ugly, virtuous, and foolish," this did not prevent her husband being jealous of her. He abused her, kicked and beat her, and dragged her about with him from place to place at all hours of the day and night. His own habits were most eccentric: he had always four dinners ready for him at his various country-houses—

but, Saint Simon says, none of them cost him much. Some soup and half a roast chicken was all that he ever ordered at each place.

In his earlier days he had been the Lothario of the Court, and we are told that the stories of his intrigues and love adventures would fill volumes. He would put on every sort of disguise to make his way to the fair lady of the hour. He spent millions on the Marchioness of Richelieu, and on one occasion hired the whole side of one of the streets near Saint Sulpice, furnished the houses, and then broke down the connecting walls to reach the place of rendezvous.

There was no end to the freaks he played on his unfortunate neighbours. One of them, by name Rose, refused to sell him a park that adjoined his property, whereupon M. le Prince turned three or four hundred foxes loose across the boundary walls of the estate. "You may imagine," says Saint Simon, "the disorder caused by this band of marauders, and the extreme surprise of Rose and his people at this inexhaustible swarm of foxes that had sprung up in a single night." Rose, however, was a man of spirit, and complained to the king, and his tormentor had to apologise, clear the ground of foxes, and repair damages.

In his later years M. le Prince was subject to all kinds of hallucinations. He fancied himself a dog, and would bark and snap at his valets; then he thought himself dead, and was with some difficulty persuaded by his doctor that dead men occasionally eat and drank. Some obliging persons were induced to pretend themselves to be dead, in order to get M. le Prince to eat his dinner in their company, and the "dialogues des morts" that took place on these occasions nearly made his doctor expire with laughter. At last, to every one's great relief, in 1709, M. le Prince died in real earnest. "Not a soul regretted him; neither servants, nor friends, nor children, nor wife." Madame la Princesse—the poor, little, ugly, forsaken woman—did indeed shed some tears, but apologised for her inconsistency in doing so.

"M. le Duc," who succeeded to the family honours, only survived his father some eleven months. Like the rest of Condé's descendants, he was marvellously short,— like a gnome, with a monstrous head and a projecting stomach, and a complexion of a livid yellow. "He had an air so haughty and audacious, that one could hardly get accustomed to him. . . . All the furies seemed to torment him perpetually, and to make him as terrible as those wild animals which appear to be only created to devour and make war upon the human race." Even his pleasantry took a dangerous turn, and his guests at Chantilly lived in terror of their lives. He threw a plate at Count Fiesque's head for venturing to contradict him at table; and he poisoned Santeuil (a good-natured writer of *vers de société*) by emptying a box of Spanish snuff into his champagne-glass—"to see what the effect of it would be."[1] It was not long, adds Saint Simon, before he was enlightened, for the unfortunate poet died the same evening in horrible agony.

[1] This was not the first time that Santeuil had suffered from the high spirits of his fine friends at Chantilly. One evening at supper, Madame la Duchesse, affronted at some real or supposed neglect of his, boxed his ears, and then, on his looking angry, threw a glass of water in his face, observing pleasantly that it was only the rain after the thunder.

It is pleasant to turn from M. le Duc to Madame la Duchesse (a daughter of Louis by Madame de Montespan). Although Saint Simon both feared and hated her—and with some reason, as we shall see hereafter—he cannot help admiring her, and he has described her as "the queen of pleasure and delight, . . . with a figure formed by the tenderest loves," and "with all the charms and all the dangers of the siren of the poets;" loving no one, and known to love no one, yet irresistible even with those who most hated her; yet, with all her attractions, cruel, heartless, and implacable—a faithless friend and a relentless enemy. How she reigned over the society at Meudon, and how she domineered over Monseigneur, will be told in another chapter.

CHAPTER VI.

MADAME DE MAINTENON.

MADAME DE MAINTENON is still the same *femme incom‑prise* that she was in her own day. No two critics agree in their estimate of her life and character. We have two pictures of her so utterly unlike, that they seem to describe two different persons; the popular one, drawn by Voltaire and Saint Simon, representing her as utterly false and unscrupulous, cruel and bigoted, a heartless adventuress—while from the other canvas there smiles upon us the gracious and beneficent foundress of Saint Cyr, the devoted wife, and the much-enduring and much-maligned keeper of the royal conscience. Which of these two portraits is the truer one, must be left to higher authorities to determine; but, even taking her as we find her, on the evidence of her own letters, and accepting all that her apologists have found to say in her favour, we can only conclude, with Madame du Deffand, in conceiving "a high opinion of her mind, little esteem for her heart, and no taste for her person; but a thorough belief in her sincerity." Those again who read Saint Simon's account of her, must remember that, in her case, he is the most partial and prejudiced of witnesses. He hated her so intensely, that if she had possessed all the virtues and all the graces that ever fell to the lot of woman, she would still have been to him the widow Scarron who had made herself a queen. He never mentions her name without adding some term of abuse—"a creole," "an old sorceress," "an obscure and artful maid-servant," "a woman of the streets." Indeed he proves too much against his enemy. Had she been all that he says she was—a false and selfish *intriguante*, mean, narrow-minded, and thoroughly unscrupulous, "consistent only in her love of power"—she could hardly have been honoured and almost idolised by a prince like Louis, with his strong common-sense and keen insight into character. Saint Simon would say that he was bewitched by this enchantress. Yes; but would the charm have lasted thirty years? During all these years we find nothing but the most devoted respect and attachment on one side, and the most unwearied care and solicitude on the other. If Madame de Maintenon was nothing better than Becky Sharp on a grander scale, surely time must have found her out. An adventuress cannot keep on the mask for ever.

But putting her character aside for the present, no romance ever contained incidents so strange as the realities of her life. The daughter of a broken spendthrift—"*peut-être gentilhomme*," says Saint Simon—born in a prison on a foreign island; so sickly as an infant, that she was once nearly thrown into the sea for dead on the homeward voyage; then left a penniless orphan, and earning her livelihood as a half-starved drudge in a relative's household,—feeding the poultry and measuring out the corn; then imprisoned in a convent, and persecuted by nuns and priests to change her creed; afterwards married out of pity by Scarron, a crippled and deformed buffoon-rhymester (*cul-de-jatte*), but in a few years left a widow in the prime of her beauty, and thrown upon the world without money and without position,—such was the story, briefly told, of the early life of Francoise d'Aubigné, afterwards known in history as Madame de Maintenon.

Saint Simon hints at scandals connected with her life in the days of her widowhood; indeed he names several of her more favoured admirers, and the fact of her intimate friendship with Ninon de l'Enclos certainly tells against her.[1] But in this point her very faults probably saved her from temptation. She was too cold, too selfish,—" trop gauche pour l'amour," as Ninon said,[1]—and too greedy of reputation, ever to give way to any warmer feeling than that of sentiment. She could nurse a sick friend, she could sympathise with sorrow, she could compassionate suffering, she could devote herself to children, she could write charming letters brimful of tears and sensibility,—but she was incapable of love. For the one absorbing idea of her life was, that all men should speak well of her; and she set herself to work to please and fascinate the society in which she found herself at the Hôtel d'Albret and the Hotel Richelieu, just as she afterwards made it her business first to captivate and

[1] M. Feuillet de Conches has in his possession the original of a letter, written by Ninon to Saint Evremond, which ends thus: "S. [Scarron] estoit mon amy; sa fame m'a donné mille plaisirs par sa conversation et, dans le tems, je l'ai trouvé trop gauche pour l'amour. Quant aux details, je ne scay rien, mais je lui ai prestay souvent ma chambre jaune à elle et à Villarseaux"—Causeries d'un Curieux, ii. 588.

then to interest and amuse her royal husband. In one of her letters she tells us the secret of her popularity in these days. "Women liked me," she says, "because I was pleasant in company, and troubled myself more about others than myself; and men followed me because I had the beauty and the grace of youth. Indeed, the taste they had for me was more in the way of a general friendship than love." So charming did she make herself, that her confessor once ordered her "to be wearisome in society" by way of penance.

But all this time, in spite of her fine friends and social distinctions, she was fighting a hard battle against poverty. Scarron's death had left her with little more than the four traditional *louis d'or* which she is said to have brought him by way of dowry; and the pension which the poet had received from the Government, was refused to his widow. She had barely sufficient money to buy food and clothing. At last, in 1664, came the crisis of her life. She happened to meet Madame de Montespan—the reigning sultana—at the Hotel d'Albret, and the great lady was so charmed with her new acquaintance that she prevailed on Louis to grant her a pension. Soon afterwards "the widow Scarron" was appointed governess to Montespan's children, secretly borne by her to the king; and as a reward for the unceasing care and devotion with which she reared them from infancy to childhood, she received the estate and title of Maintenon. But in these days Louis regarded her with little favour. His presents to her had been made on the express condition that he should never see or hear of her again: "the creature," as he called his future wife, "was insufferable," and he had already given her far more than she deserved. The first sign of his prejudice giving way was the pleasure he showed in reading some of her letters, giving an account of his children's health, and their visits to various watering-places; and, even on the most trivial subjects, few writers (as Saint Simon is obliged to admit) could express themselves so simply, so pleasantly, and yet so eloquently.[1] Then by degrees his Majesty found that the lady could talk even more pleasantly than she wrote; that there was a *solidité* about her conversation rarely found among her frivolous sex; that her temper never varied; that her manners had an incomparable charm; and that her intelligence and good sense soothed and refreshed him after all he had endured from the moods and humours of Madame de Montespan. And thus by degrees she became necessary to his comfort and convenience; he resorted to her for assistance in his doubts and difficulties; she almost took the place of his confessor; she lectured him on the frailties of his past life; and the two would sit for hours together, evening after evening,—she talking earnestly and gravely, while he listened to her in rapt attention.

Other circumstances contributed to increase her influence. Louis had passed the prime of life, and time had sobered the strong passions of his youth. Warnings, moreover, had come to him in various shapes. His

---

[1] Napoleon read her letters at St Helena, and said of them, "The style, the grace, the purity of the language enchant me. I think I prefer them to those of Madame de Sévigné — they tell you more (*elles vous disent plus de choses*)."

Madame de Maintenon left fourteen volumes of letters behind her, and a complete edition of them is now being edited by M. Théophile Lavallée—complete, that is, as she left them; but she seems to have herself purposely destroyed many of the most important.

confessor had reminded him of the scandal and danger of living in mortal sin; Bourdaloue had not scrupled to apply to him, from the pulpit, the story of David and Uriah; and the sight of his last victim, Fontanges, a girl of eighteen, dying suddenly and miserably, touched him with keen remorse, and served to complete the good work begun by Madame de Maintenon. At length Madame de Montespan, although furious with indignation at being so treacherously supplanted by an "elderly governess," as she called her rival, saw herself that her reign was over, and she finally left Versailles in 1686, never to return.

Saint Simon touches on Montespan's subsequent history with what is for him an unusually gentle hand. "It was years," he says, "before she could accustom herself to a life of retreat. She carried her leisure and restlessness about with her from place to place. At last God touched her heart. Her sin had never been accompanied by forgetfulness. She used often to leave the king, to pray in her own chamber." And now it seemed as if no penance and humiliation could be too severe — the roughest clothing or the coarsest food; but perhaps the most terrible atonement of all was that insisted on by her confessor — to ask her husband to receive her again on any terms. She wrote him a humble letter, as she was bidden; but his only answer was, that he neither wished to see her face nor hear her name again.

Still, even in her retirement, she seems to have been a person much sought after. Her house was filled incessantly by a stream of visitors. "All France used to go there," says Saint Simon, "and she received her guests with the air and manner of a queen, . . .

beautiful as the day to the last hour of her life;" still charming all hearers with that graceful play of wit peculiar to her family, and known as the *esprit de Mortemart;* and still occasionally indulging in sallies of that ridicule which had formerly so keen an edge, that the courtiers avoided her windows at Versailles if she was standing in the balcony, for it was worse (so they said) than passing under a drawn sword. Like other fair penitents, Montespan apparently found it easier to mortify her body than to curb her tongue.

Although always in excellent health, the fear of death haunted her continually. She even paid women to sit up all night long in her bedroom, and kept candles burning at the windows while she slept. But when death came upon her at last, these terrors disappeared, and she died with the most perfect resignation. Shortly before she expired, Antin, her only legitimate son, arrived and asked to see his mother. With the heartlessness that seems to have been his second nature, he looked at her curiously and coldly for a few moments, wished her farewell, and scarcely waited till she breathed her last. He gave some directions about her funeral, and then galloped off to hunt with his friend Monseigneur. Her other children showed a more natural feeling, and mourned for her with some sincerity; but (Saint Simon tells us) it was the poor people in her neighbourhood, on whom she had lavished half her fortune in her latter years, who showed the most genuine sorrow. Madame de Maintenon shed tears when she heard the news— tears of remorse, Saint Simon thinks; but the king, for whom Montespan had sacrificed her happiness and honour, showed such indifference, that even the Duchess of Burgundy expressed surprise that her death had not affected him more. "She has been dead to me," he replied, "ever since I bade her farewell years ago."

Meanwhile fortune seemed to smile upon Montespan's successful rival. In 1683 the queen, Maria Theresa, died—happy, perhaps, in being at last released from a life of sorrow and neglect. Forced always to ignore the infidelities of her husband, she had been grateful for the smallest kindness, and especially for the consideration always shown her by Madame de Maintenon. "I believe," said the poor woman, "that God raised her up to give me back the heart that Madame de Montespan had robbed me of. Never have I been so well treated by the king as from the day he first listened to her." Not only did she give the Marchioness a portrait of herself, set in diamonds; but on her deathbed she drew off her signet-ring and put it on Madame de Maintenon's hand, thus giving her, as it were, a right of succession. The Marchioness was then leaving the room, when the Duke of Rochefoucauld stopped her. "This is not the time to leave the king," said he; "you must stay, for his Majesty has need of you;" and she stayed accordingly.

That she was actually married to Louis before two years had elapsed there can be no reasonable doubt. Voltaire speaks of their marriage as a well-known fact; and Saint Simon says that Bontems, the king's valet, among other marks of confidence, had been intrusted with the arrangement of the midnight Mass held in the winter of 1685, when the Archbishop of Paris solemnised their marriage before a few witnesses. Indeed the marriage would have been made public the next day had not Louvois gone on his knees before Louis, and implored him not to disgrace himself in the eyes of Europe. But, whether acknowledged or not, Saint Simon does not conceal his own belief that, in celebrating this marriage at all, Louis had sealed his own doom.

"Thus it was that Providence prepared for the proudest of kings the profoundest, the most public, the most lasting, and the most unheard-of humiliation. .. . . . All that resulted—her triumph, his entire confidence in her, his rare dependence on her, her absolute power, the public and universal adoration paid her by Ministers, generals, the royal family—all, in a word, at her feet; everything good and lucky obtained through her, and everything refused unless she asked it; men, affairs of state, patronage, justice, favour, religion—everything without exception was in her hands, and the king and the state were her victims. What kind of woman she was, this incredible enchantress, and how she governed without a break, without an obstacle, without the slightest cloud, for more than thirty whole years—this is the incomparable spectacle which it concerns us to retrace, as it has long since concerned the whole of Europe."

From this year, 1685, Madame de Maintenon was Queen of France in all but the name, and no queen in history was ever so exclusive or difficult of access. Her room at Versailles was a sanctuary to which none were admitted but the royal family, the Ministers of State, and a few intimate friends. Saint Simon himself probably never set foot across the threshold, and all he knew of its mistress was from some of the more privileged courtiers. In this room Madame de Maintenon remained the whole day when she was not at Saint Cyr, enshrined in what she called her "niche"—a three-cornered sofa of red damask; and here she received her visitors, always seated herself, and never rising even to receive the Queen of England when she came over from Saint Germains to call on her. Occasionally, when Louis had no work with his Ministers, select dinners, sometimes followed by music or theatricals, took place in her apartment; but ordinarily the Ministers would bring their portfolios after dinner, and the king would work for hours while Madame de Maintenon sat at her embroidery listening to the discussion, but never volunteering her advice, knowing that, as a matter of fact, it would always be asked sooner or later. "*Que pense-t-en Votre Solidité?*" Louis would sometimes ask in a bantering manner. She would smile, says Saint Simon, pretend utter ignorance, talk of something else, but eventually led back the conversation to the point she wished to carry, or to the name of the person she wished to favour. But she could not always calculate on getting what she asked, and sometimes met with a rebuff that made her shed tears at the time, and kept her on thorns for days afterwards. Even the most favoured Minister could never make certain that his petition for some particular candidate would not meet with an abrupt refusal.

"'You do not know how the land lies,' said one of them to a friend. 'Of twenty matters that we bring before the king, we are certain that he will pass nineteen as we wish; but we are equally certain that the twentieth will be decided against us. Which of these twenty will be decided against our wish and desire is what we can never tell, and very often it is just that matter in which we are most interested. The king reserves this stroke (*bisque*) to make us feel that he is master, and that it is he who reigns; and if by chance something is proposed about which he has a strong opinion, and which is sufficiently important for us to have an opinion about it as well, either on account of the thing itself or for the desire we have that it should succeed—it is very often then, in the rare event of its happening, that we are certain to get well scolded (*une sortie sûre*); but as a matter of fact, when the scolding is over, and the affair fallen through, the king—content with having shown us that we are powerless, and sorry to have annoyed us — becomes supple, and *then* comes the time when we can do all we want.'"

As an instance of Madame de Maintenon's power, Saint Simon tells us that even her old servant Nanon, who had followed her fortunes from first to last, was always embraced by the princesses, and saluted with profound bows by the Ministers; and when the Duchess de Lude wished for the post of Maid of Honour to the young Duchess of Burgundy, she sent her maid with twenty thousand crowns to Nanon, as the simplest way of gaining her object, and the same evening she was gazetted to the post. "So it is with Courts," our author moralises; "a Nanon sells the most important and brilliant offices of state; and a rich lady—a Duchess of noble birth, without children or ties of any kind, but free and her own mistress—is foolish enough to sell herself into slavery at such a price."

One memorable scene is recorded by Saint Simon as showing the profound respect with which Madame de Maintenon was always treated by the king in public. "He would have been a hundred times freer with the queen, and shown far less gallantry." The occasion was the camp at Compiègne in 1698,—one of those magnificent displays of mimic warfare in which Louis delighted. Even Saint Simon's usual command of language almost fails him when he tries to describe the full splendour of the spectacle—"so startling, so entrancing, one must say so frightfully gorgeous"—the avenues of tents covered with tapestry and strewn with carpets, the ranges of kitchens and stables, the aqueducts fifty miles long which brought water for the immense host, the roads blocked with endless trains of pack-horses and sumpter-mules, the crowds of camp-followers, the musicians and pastry-cooks, the tailors and wig-makers, the banquets served on gold and silver plate, to supply which the neighbouring forests were ransacked for game and venison, and the seas for fish; and then the splendour of the review itself, when sixty thousand picked troops exercised, manœuvred, and went through all the details of a regular campaign under the eyes of Louis and his Court.

"But a spectacle of another sort, that I could paint forty years hence as well as to-day, so strongly did it impress me, was that which, from the summit of this rampart, the king presented to all his army and to the innumerable crowd of spectators of all kinds in the plain below.

"Madame de Maintenon sat alone, in her sedan-chair, facing the plain and the troops, between its three windows drawn up, her porters having retired to a distance. On the left pole in front sat the Duchess of Burgundy, and on the same side, standing in a semicircle, were Madame la Duchesse, the Princess of Conti, and all the ladies, and behind them again there were some men. At the right window was the king, standing, and a little in the rear a semicircle of the most distinguished men of the Court. The king was nearly always uncovered, and every now and then stooped to speak to Madame de Maintenon, and explain to her what she saw, and the reason of each movement. Each time that he did so she was obliging enough to open the window four or five inches, but never half-way, for I took particular notice, and I admit that I was more attentive to this spectacle than to that of the troops. Sometimes she opened the glasses of her own accord to ask some question of him, but generally it was he who, without waiting for her, stooped down to explain to her what was passing; and sometimes, if she did not notice him, he tapped at the glass to make her open it. He never spoke save to her, except when he gave a few brief orders, or just answered the Duchess of Burgundy, who wanted to make him speak, and with whom Madame de Maintenon carried on a conversation by signs without opening the front window, through which the young princess screamed a few words at her now and then. I carefully watched the faces of the bystanders. All showed an embarrassed, timid, and stealthy surprise; every one behind the chair and in the semicircle watched this scene more than what was going on in the army. The king often put his hat on the top of the chair in order to get his head in to speak, and this continual exercise tired his loins very much. Monseigneur was on horseback in the plain with the young princes. It was about five o'clock in the afternoon, and the weather was as brilliant as could be desired.

. . . .

"About the time when the town capitulated, Madame de Maintenon apparently asked permission to go away, for the king called out, 'The chairmen of Madame!' They came and took her away; in less than a quarter of an hour afterwards the king retired also, and nearly everybody else. Many spoke with their eyes and nudged one another as they went off, or whispered in their neighbour's ear. Everybody was full of what had taken place on the ramparts between the king and Madame de Maintenon. Even the soldiers asked the meaning of that sedan-chair, and of the king every moment stooping to put his head inside of it. It became necessary gently to silence these questions on the part of the troops. What effect this sight had upon foreigners present, and what they said of it, may be imagined. All over

Europe it was as much talked of as the camp of Compiègne itself, with all its pomp and prodigious splendour."

Although her ambition was satisfied, it may be questioned if Madame de Maintenon knew any real happiness in these days of her power, except in the seclusion of Saint Cyr. Her sin — the "*péché de Lucifer*," of which she speaks — assuredly brought its own penalty. "Who knows," she writes, "whether I am not punished by the very excess of my prosperity? Who knows whether, rightly interpreted, the language of Providence to me is not this, 'You have desired honour and glory; you shall have them to satiety'?" Her letters are full of expressions of the weariness which preyed upon her continually. One day, looking at some fish that were restless and ill at ease in a marble tank—"They are like me," she said; "they long to get back to their mud:" and again, as she heard a young girl singing—"Tell me," she asked her ladies, "is not Jeannette's lot a happier one than mine?"

In one remarkable letter[1] she has described her long and weary day at Versailles, and tells how from seven in the morning till ten at night her room was filled by a succession of visitors going and coming; how all the jealousies and discontents of her friends were poured into her ears; how the women talked scandal and the men talked politics; how princes and Ministers pestered her alike; how she had to entertain Monseigneur, who never originated an idea himself, and to cheer and

---

[1] This interesting letter is given at length by M. Chéruel in his work on Saint Simon, p. 509. It will be found in Lavallée's edition of Madame de Maintenon's Letters, ii. 156.

console Louis, who would come back from his day's hunting melancholy and dispirited; and how, when the evening came, she was often so fatigued herself that she could hold out no longer, and had to seek refuge in her bed; but even then she could not sleep from sheer weariness of mind and body.

Louis himself never spared her, any more than he spared the other ladies of his Court.

"I have seen her," says Saint Simon, "travel from Marly or Fontainebleau so dangerously ill that one could not tell whether she would not die on the road. But, whatever her state might be, the king would come to her room at the usual hour, attended by his suite, without thought or care. It has often happened that he has thus come in while she was in the agonies of a feverish attack, and ordered all the windows to be opened, if he found them shut, to let in the air. If he required cards or music, her headache or any other infirmity was no hindrance. She must endure it all without complaint, and with a hundred candles flaring in her eyes."

Then she had other vexations. Her brother, D'Aubigné, was a constant source of annoyance to her. He was always in debt and difficulties, and many of her letters are addressed to him urging prudence and economy. He was only a captain in the Guards, but complained that he ought to have been a marshal at least: "However," as he said once to some one who wondered how he could afford to play for such high stakes, "he had taken out his baton in money." Then he married badly, and things got worse. At last Madame de Maintenon persuaded him to go into a kind of retreat for decayed gentlemen near Saint Sulpice; but D'Aubigné found this life so intolerably dull that he made his escape into Paris, where he relapsed into his old habits. Finally, Madame de Maintenon, in despair, put him under the charge of "the stupidest priest in Saint Sulpice," who followed him everywhere like a shadow, and made his life a burden to him. Saint Simon says D'Aubigné was a good, honest fellow, very different from his sister, and that it was the best fun in the world to hear him talk of the king "his brother-in-law," and of the "widow Scarron" of former days.

Saint Cyr was only a few miles from Versailles,— dangerously near, as some people thought, like a dove-cot near a hawk's nest,—and in its lecture-rooms and gardens Madame de Maintenon would pass whole days, when she could be spared from Court, playing that "*rôle* of Mentor and Minerva," which was her second nature; directing, observing, advising, teaching classes, and surrounded by the young girls, whom she encouraged to talk and question her; telling them stories of her past life and of the world outside their walls, or writing tales and conversations to amuse them. Of this busy side of her life she never grew wearied. "Nothing," she writes, "is dearer to me than my children at Saint Cyr. I love the whole place, even to the dust beneath their feet."

By way of giving them ease and refinement of manner, some of the elder girls were taught to act scenes from "Cinna" and "Andromache;" but in the latter piece (there are four lovers in it) they seem to have overdone their parts, and Madame de Maintenon writes in consequence to Racine: "Our girls have just acted 'Andromache,' and have acted it so well that they shall never act it again, or any other of your pieces;" and she requires him to write something moral, serious, and historical—" with no love in it." Racine obeyed, and wrote "Esther," with which Madame de Maintenon was charmed,—not so much by the beauty of the words as by the scarcely-veiled allegory which made her the chaste and modest Jewish maiden who triumphs over the imperious Vashti (Montespan) and the disgraced Aman (Louvois), and becomes the bride of the great and beneficent Ahasuerus (Louis). The piece was acted again and again, and on one occasion Madame de Sévigné was present, and says, "The harmony between the music, verses, hymns, and personages of the drama was so perfect as to leave nothing to be desired. All was simple, innocent, sublime, and touching, and the hymns were of a beauty not to be listened to without tears."

It was to Saint Cyr that Madame de Maintenon retired, "after seeing," as she said, "the king die like a saint and a hero;" and it was here that she found the rest and repose she had, by her own account, longed for all her life. She lived in the completest retirement—reading and writing, frequently attending Mass, receiving the visits of a few friends, and almost forgotten by the world. She was well provided for by the liberal pension allowed her by the Regent, "which her disinterestedness had made necessary;" and, Saint Simon adds, "no abbess, no daughter of France, was so absolute, so punctually obeyed, so feared, so respected, and at the same time so loved, as she was by all immured within Saint Cyr."

We only once hear of her retreat being disturbed, and that was on the occasion of the Czar's visit to Paris in 1717. When she heard he was coming to see her, Madame de Maintenon went to bed at once, as the safest place of refuge; but she was not safe even there. The Czar entered her room, and, with the rudeness of his nation, drew aside the curtains of her bed and told his interpreter to ask her what her sickness was. "A great age" (*une grande vieillese*) was the reply; and then, after a prolonged stare, his Majesty withdrew without a word, and she was left in peace.[1] It is almost the last time that her name appears in history. She died at the age of eighty-three, listening to the hymns of her favourite pupils, and was buried in the chapel attached to the convent. "Your house shall never fail you," she had once written to the Abbess, "so long as there shall be a king of France;" and up till 1793 her prophecy held good. But in that year the storm of the Revolution broke upon Saint Cyr: the teachers and pupils were dispersed, the cloisters desecrated, and the body of the foundress was torn from its coffin. By the pious care of her relation, the Duke of Noailles, her remains were afterwards restored to their former resting-place, and a simple slab of black marble may still be seen, let into the wall of the chapel, with the modest inscription—

CY GÎT MADAME DE MAINTENON
1635 · 1719 · 1836.

---

[1] This is the ordinary account; but Saint Simon says, "The Czar said not a word to her nor she to him."

CHAPTER VII.

SAINT SIMON'S LIFE AT COURT.

ENOUGH has been already said to show that Saint Simon would find himself in troubled waters at Court. In fact, if we except the two old Dukes of Beauvilliers and Chevreuse, there was scarcely a nobleman at Versailles whom he could call his friend. He could not dissociate their personal qualities from what he considered their degraded position. What good thing could be hoped or looked for from men whose highest ambition it was to hold the king's stirrup when he mounted his horse, or hand him the towel when he had washed his hands? What could be expected from peers of lower degree, when the grandest of grand seigneurs—the Duke of Rochefoucauld—regarded it as the glory of his life never to have slept for a single night away from Versailles for forty years? The great names of history had been tarnished in the persons of their degenerate descendants. Their very titles had lost their proud significance. "Those of Count and Marquis," he says, "have been dragged in the dust by the number of these nobodies, without an acre of land, who have usurped them, and hence they have fallen away to nothing; so much so that even people of distinction, who are Marquis or Count, are absurd enough (if they will allow me to say so) to be annoyed when one gives them their title in addressing them."

Besides losing their ancestral prestige, the nobility had also lost their political influence; indeed they regarded politics as beneath their notice, and only fit for the sons of tradesmen and lawyers like Colbert and Le Tellier. "They had to choose between the desk and the sword," says Saint Simon, "and they had chosen the latter. . . . They were given up to ignorance, to frivolity, to pleasure, to foolish extravagance,—of no use on earth except to get killed in battle, and to stagnate all the rest of their time in the most deadly idleness."[1] One day, as Saint Simon was declaiming in his usual fashion against the degradation of his own order, in the presence of his friends, the two old dukes—

"'They let me talk on,' he says, 'for some time. At last the Duke of Beauvilliers got very red, and asked me in a severe tone, 'What is it, then, you wish for yourself that would content you?'

"'I will tell you, sir,' I answered, warmly; 'I should like to be born of a good old family; to have a fine estate also, with fine privileges attached to it, without dreaming of being extremely rich. I should be ambitious of being raised to the first dignity of my own part of the country; I should like, besides, some important office at Court; to enjoy all that; and then—I should be content.'

"The two dukes listened to me, looked at one another, smiled, said nothing in reply, and a moment afterwards purposely changed the subject."

---

[1] In the same way De Tocqueville considers one of the proximate causes of the French Revolution to have been the "useless, idle, and restless lives passed by the *noblesse*," who had retained their feudal privileges without their political power.—(See his essay in the 'Westminster Review' of 1836, and Ancien Regime, p. 151.)

The sublime egotism of these aspirations, and the frankness with which he confides them to his friends—and to us—are highly characteristic of Saint Simon. This personal vein pervades almost every chapter. His own views, his own ideas, his own theories — how he lectured this friend, and how he denounced that enemy —what he thought of the Bull *Unigenitus*, what he wrote on the training of the Dauphin, what he said on almost every subject of the day,—all this, while it gives to his Memoirs an interest and individuality of their own, certainly goes far to justify Marmontel's criticism — that Saint Simon " saw nothing in the nation but the Nobility; nothing in the Nobility but the Dukes and Peers; and nothing in the Dukes and Peers but HIMSELF."

His lawsuit against Luxemburg [1] was only the prelude to a series of attacks upon some of the proudest titles in the French peerage. Amongst others, the Lorraines had incurred his deadly enmity by what he calls their "*tracasseries.*" The Duke of Lorraine had married " Mademoiselle," daughter of " Monsieur," the king's brother, and had assumed a ducal coronet, with the royal fleur-de-lys, and had even claimed the title of " Royal Highness " from the people in his duchy. Besides these acts of insolence, the ladies of the family had refused to carry round the alms-plate in the chapel —as if they were of the blood-royal. Then the other Court ladies began to think the duty undignified ; and at last none of the duchesses, including Madame de Saint Simon, would undertake it. The king expressed his displeasure at this frivolous dispute, thinking, with some justice, that Saint Simon was the cause of it all.

[1] See p. 35.

"Since he had left the army," he complained, "he had done nothing but study questions of precedence; and it would serve him right if he were to banish him from Court altogether."

This thunder from Olympus alarmed Saint Simon, and he at once obtained an audience of the king, when he explained and apologised for himself. Had he had any idea that he was offending his Majesty, he "would have carried round the plate himself, like a village churchwarden." The disturbance, he declared, was entirely owing to the Lorraines — more especially to "M. le Grand," Louis de Lorraine, then sixty years of age, who was a personal friend of the king's, and, even by Saint Simon's own showing, the greatest nobleman at the Court. To quarrel with him was almost like flying in the face of royalty itself.

He seems, however, for the time, to have made his peace with the king, for, not very long after the "Affair of the Alms-Rate," he was, to his great surprise, nominated Ambassador to Rome—a high honour for a young duke of thirty. But such an appointment then, as now, involved considerable expense, and Saint Simon was in doubt as to whether he could afford to accept it. His friends, however, strongly advised his doing so—he might take it without being absolutely ruined, the Chancellor told him; and his wife gave him the same advice.

He takes this opportunity of telling us of the high compliment paid by the Ministers on this occasion to his wife's good sense, and how they advised him to keep nothing secret from her in his embassy—"to have her at the end of the table when he wrote and read despatches, and to ask her opinion on all occasions." He says that he always did so, and never found any one's advice so wise, so judicious, and so useful.

But Saint Simon never went as ambassador to Rome after all. The appointment was cancelled a few days after it was announced—to his wife's (and possibly to his own) great relief; and he attributes this blow to his dignity to his enemies at Court, and, above all, "to the strange aversion of Madame de Maintenon." His very virtues, he declares, had told against him in this matter. Louis was jealous of a young man reported to be not only "a boaster, a grumbler, and full of theories," but besides, "to have talent, learning, capacity, and application,—in short, to have every quality necessary to a statesman" (*homme enfin très propre aux affaires*). Thus, while men far inferior to him intellectually, but more adroit courtiers, were daily receiving fresh honours and appointments,—pensions, and governorships, and abbeys, and preferments of every kind,—Saint Simon found himself left out in the cold, unnoticed and undistinguished. Nor did his position improve as time went on. Instead of making the attempt to swim with the stream, and conciliate his opponents, he seems to have continually made fresh enemies. Not content with attacking the Lorraines, and other peers, on questions of precedence, he embroiled himself with the "Meudon cabal"[1] (the Dauphin's set); he made two bitter personal enemies in Antin and the Duke of Maine—the ablest and most popular men of the rising generation—and he gave great offence to Louis by betting five pistoles with some boastful courtier that the fortress of Lille would be taken by the enemy before it could be relieved by Vendôme. As

[1] See p. 147.

he confesses, it was a rash and foolish wager, that ought never to have been made; and as the fact of the fortress surrendering, after a heroic defence, increased the king's prejudice against this young duke, who seemed to be as unpatriotic as he was free of speech, Saint Simon soon paid the penalty for his imprudence, and indeed began to find his position at Court so embarrassing, with enemies and calumniators on all sides of him, that he determined for a time to leave Versailles altogether, and, as he says, "to breathe a healthier and more peaceful air" at his country seat.

There he was joined by Chamillart, the disgraced Foreign Minister, who had been, like his friend, attacked by some of the Dauphin's clique at Meudon, and who had been too proud or too honest to stoop to conciliate them. Saint Simon tells us how serenely and cheerfully Chamillart bore his change of fortune, but notices that he would never be alone for a moment if he could help it—"like a man who fears himself, and seeks to fill the void he feels in his own heart."

After Chamillart had left, Saint Simon still stayed on at La Ferté; indeed he had some idea of settling down there altogether, but his wife, with her usual good sense, pointed out the absurdity of his thus burying himself in the country, where he would soon get tired of his books and solitary walks. His friend Pontchartrain (the Chancellor) took the same view, and it ended in Saint Simon's returning to Versailles.

He was greatly struck, on his return, by the isolated position of his old friend and comrade, the Duke of Orleans. This prince, who had always been more or less out of favour at Court, had lately given mortal offence to two powerful ladies, Madame de Maintenon and the Princess des Ursins, by styling them, in an after-dinner speech, "the She-Captain" and "She-Lieutenant" of France. The sting of this jest lay in its evident truth, and both these women determined to revenge themselves on the perpetrator of this "fatal *bon-mot*." It was not difficult to injure Orleans's reputation, for it was already sufficiently bad. He was said to have conspired against the Spanish Crown—to have intended to divorce (if not poison) his own wife, then marry the sister-in-law of the late King of Spain, and then imitate the unnatural conduct of William III. of England, by dethroning his near relative, the Duke of Anjou. A storm of indignation had broken out. Even Monseigneur had been roused from his usual apathy, and had demanded that Orleans should be impeached on a charge of conspiracy and high treason. This proposal was seriously debated in the Cabinet, and the Chancellor privately asked Saint Simon what would be the proper form of impeachment in such a case. Saint Simon, however, assured him that the high treason, if committed at all, was against Spain, not France, and that the accused must accordingly be tried by a Spanish, and not by a French, tribunal.

Saint Simon next resolved to rescue Orleans, if possible, from his degraded and isolated position at Court, and, as a first step, to break off his *liaison* with a Madlle. de Sèry (afterwards known as Madame d'Argenton)—the Phyllis, without whom he declared, in some very indifferent verses, life would be insupportable. To break off this connection was a difficult as well as a delicate task; and those sixty pages, in which

Saint Simon tells us how powerfully he worked upon the better feelings of the prince, contain some of the finest passages in his Memoirs. He placed before Orleans "the choice of Hercules" over again — but clothed in language that might have come from the lips of Bossuet or Bourdaloue. He enlarged on the great possibilities of the future, to a prince of the rank and position occupied by Orleans, "on the steps of the throne itself;" he placed on one hand the lustre and brilliancy of a life devoted to high and noble purposes, the honour of his country, the esteem of his peers, the confidence of his sovereign,—and on the other side he draws a hideous picture of nobles "whom their birth, their family, their establishment, and their dignity should naturally have carried to the distinctions due to their position, degraded by their debauchery, unknown at Court, abandoned to their own proper shame and misery, scorned even by the vilest company, objects of censure and contempt to king and people, reduced to such a state of degradation as to be not worth correction or reproof"—and then he names several characters who had been thus "buried in the slime." It now rested with Orleans himself, his mentor concludes, "to choose once and for all his life one of these two states—so different—lying ready to his hands, since, after so many wasted years, another step on the downward road would seal the stone of the sepulchre where he would be immured alive, and whence no human aid could possibly draw him forth." And then, with a reference to the "prodigious mischief which would be caused to the State by the loss of a prince of his rank, of his age, and of his talents," Saint Simon brings his long harangue to a close.

Orleans was so profoundly moved, as well he might be, by this "terrible after-dinner scene," that he sought an interview the same evening with Madame de Maintenon, who, to his intense surprise, told him precisely what Saint Simon had told him,—"even in the same phrases and same arrangement of sentences." He was inclined to suspect that his friend was in collusion with "that woman," as he called her; but after all, as Marshal Besons, who was present at the interview, observed, there was nothing so very strange in this coincidence, for truth must be always the same, whether it came from the lips of Saint Simon or of Madame de Maintenon.

Then Orleans had an audience of the king, but Louis had received the poor prince's expressions of penitence with so cold and stern an air, that Orleans returned from the interview in a state of despair, which alarmed his two friends. "He threw himself on a sofa, and sometimes stupefied, sometimes cruelly agitated, only expressed his feelings by an appalling silence, or by a torrent of sighs, sobs, and tears, while we were ourselves agitated and excited by such a violent paroxysm, and restrained our joy, and did not dare to speak, and could with difficulty persuade ourselves that this connection had been so fortunately broken off." A few days afterwards Madame d'Argenton left the Palais Royal, and we hear the last of her.

Saint Simon now thought it would be a good time to make his own peace if possible with Louis, and he accordingly requested a private audience in that precious half-hour between his Majesty's toilet and morning Mass, when he made what we should now call "a personal explanation." At first Louis listened with a haughty air of attention, "which gradually softened into a more open expression of kindness and satisfaction," as Saint Simon pleaded his cause with his usual fervid eloquence; and the interview ended by the king, "with a fatherly air," giving him some good-humoured advice, not to talk so much, nor to be so keen on questions of rank, and so to avoid making personal enemies: then he dismissed him with a smiling and gracious bow.

From this time Saint Simon's position at Court seems to have improved. Previously he had not even had a room at Versailles that he could call his own. That which he occupied had been lent him by his father-in-law, De Lorges. But now a suite of six rooms was allotted to him in the new wing near the chapel. Each of these rooms had a sort of cabinet at the back; and one of these cabinets was turned into what he calls his "workshop." Here were his books and papers: here in solitude and silence he could transcribe each evening the events of the day, and keep the journal on which his Memoirs were founded. Here, too, he could discuss future schemes of State policy with his friends Chevreuse or Beauvilliers without fear of interruption from unwelcome visitors; or hold such private interviews as that he has described to us with the king's confessor.

But his active mind was never at rest. No sooner had he extricated Orleans from his embarrassment, than we find him busied in contriving a marriage between Orleans's daughter, "Mademoiselle," and the Duc de Berry—son of Monseigneur, and grandson of Louis XIV., —a most difficult task, as these two branches of the royal family were scarcely on speaking terms. Moreover, the

Meudon faction had other views for Monseigneur's son. But the difficulties only served to excite Saint Simon's energies, and he made use of his intimate knowledge of the different "cabals" to play one off against the other with consummate skill. He was fortunate enough to secure the goodwill of the ladies, the Jesuits, and above all of Madame de Maintenon, and the king's confessor, Père le Tellier, whose veto would have stopped the whole business. Next he had to overcome strong opposition on the part of Monseigneur and "the Meudon faction," who hated the very name of an alliance with the Orleans branch of the Bourbons, and who wished that Monseigneur's son should marry the young daughter of "Madame la Duchesse," the head of their own society. At the first hint of the marriage projected by Saint Simon, Monseigneur, mild as he was usually, exploded with anger. Furthermore, it was necessary that Orleans should get the king's formal consent to the match; and Orleans was "as immovable as a log." It was with the greatest difficulty that he could be induced even to write a letter on the subject; and in the end Saint Simon had to write it himself, and Orleans made a fair copy of it. But, even then, Orleans kept this precious letter in his pocket a whole week without daring to deliver it; and it was only by actually pushing him by the shoulders into the royal presence that Saint Simon could induce him to present it. But the letter was given, and the king read it carefully through twice. In a few days he called Monseigneur, and told him, "with the air of a king and father," that the marriage must take place; and Monseigneur "did not dare to gainsay the king, for the first time in his life." He stammered, hesitated, and at last gave way. Indeed, after the first moments of disgust, he took the whole business easily enough; and, when Orleans and his wife came to call on him, he embraced them warmly, made them dine with him, drank their healths repeatedly, and appeared to be in the highest state of delight and good-humour.

Antin was the first of the Meudon party who heard the news, but, far from betraying the least feeling of annoyance, he even went so far as to " applaud the idea with that delicate taste of flattery which he had so largely at his command, and which cost him so little even in the things which annoyed him most." But he at once posted off a courier to Madame la Duchesse. The news fell upon her like a thunderbolt, and her rage and indignation were extreme. " I would have given a good deal," says Saint Simon, maliciously, " to have been hidden behind the tapestry in those first strange moments."

Saint Simon received nothing but thanks and congratulations on all sides, and for the time being the triumph was complete; but unluckily, so far as any domestic happiness was concerned, or any real union between the Bourbon and Orleans branches, this marriage, so eagerly and so carefully planned, proved a miserable failure. The young Duke of Berry was himself perhaps the best of the Bourbons—" the gentlest, most amiable, and most compassionate of all men;" gay and frank with the few people he knew well, but so ignorant of all subjects except hunting, that he never ventured to open his mouth before strangers, and so afraid of the king that he lost his head completely if his Majesty addressed him, and would stand "twirling his hat in his hand like a child," without being able to articulate an answer.

From the first he was devotedly attached to his wife, and for a little time she seemed to return his affection; but soon she showed her character in its true light. She despised her easy and gentle husband, ridiculed his piety, outraged and insulted him, and herself carried on intrigues that scandalised even the lax morality of her own time. "She was a model of all the vices," says Saint Simon, "excepting avarice, and was the more dangerous as she had art and talent to help her out." In pride she even surpassed her mother, the Duchess of Orleans, whom the duke always called "Madame Lucifer," and " who smiled with pleasure at the compliment."

"It is an instance," says Saint Simon, "of how in this world people work with their heads in a sack, and how human prudence and wisdom are sometimes confounded by successes which have been reasonably devised, and which turn out detestable. . . . We discovered, when too late, that we had introduced a Fury, whose only thought was how to ruin those who had settled her in life, to injure her benefactors, to make her husband and her brother-in-law [the Duke of Burgundy] quarrel, and to put herself in the power of her enemies, merely because they were also the enemies of her natural friends."

An additional source of annoyance to Saint Simon was the appointment of his wife as Lady-in-Waiting to this demon in petticoats. It was an honour that they would both have gladly declined, but they had no choice in the matter. Not only did the Orleans family eagerly desire it—possibly in the hope that Madame de Saint Simon's good example might influence this "model of all the vices"—but Madame de Maintenon and her ladies had also set their hearts on it, and the king himself approved highly of the selection. Orleans had suggested that Saint Simon might refuse, and Louis was rather disquieted by the thought: "Your friend is sometimes a little eccentric; but refuse, oh no!—not when he learns it is *my* desire."

A few days afterwards the king summoned Saint Simon to his cabinet, and after paying him many compliments, and speaking in the highest terms of his wife—"for no man in the world knew how to do this better when he chose, and above all when he was offering you some bitter pill that he wished you to swallow"—he intimated his royal wishes in the matter, and Saint Simon did not venture even to hint at disobedience.

"The king then smiled again more cheerfully, like a man who understands you well, and who is relieved at not having met with the resistance he had expected, and who is content with that sort of liberty which he has found, and which makes him better appreciate the sacrifice that he feels has been undergone, without having his own ears wounded by it. At the same time he turned his back to the wall, which he had been facing before, a little turned towards me, and in a grave and magisterial but elevated voice, said to the company: "Madame la Duchesse de Saint Simon is Lady-in-Waiting to the future Duchesse de Berry." At once there arose a chorus of approval at the choice, and of praises of the lady chosen; and the king, without speaking further, passed on to his cabinet at the back."

It may be noticed here, as in all his other audiences recorded by Saint Simon, how thoroughly Louis is master of the situation; how even this talkative and impetuous duke is overawed by the majesty of the speaker, and does not give the faintest hint of dissent or disapproval; how few and well chosen the royal words are, and how, as they are spoken, a stillness fills the air ("a silence in which you might hear an ant walk," says Saint Simon in another passage), followed by the *brouhaha* of the courtiers, the hum of mingled applause and curiosity. And it is impossible not to be struck by the kingliness of Louis, so "bien royale," as Sainte Beuve says, even in his slightest actions; the curious thing being, that the very man who personally disliked the king so intensely, should throughout his pages bear unwilling, or perhaps unconscious, testimony to that commanding and majestic deportment which, more than any other of his kingly qualities, gained him the title of "Le Grand Monarque."

CHAPTER VIII.

JESUITS AND JANSENISTS.

WITH Madame de Maintenon began a new era in French history—the reign of the saints, or the "Cabals of the Devout," as Saint Simon calls them. The same mania for direction that had led her to found Saint Cyr, induced her also to act the part of "a universal abbess—a mother of the Church." It gratified her pride to be consulted by theologians and doctors of divinity; to correspond with cardinals and bishops; to have priests and abbés waiting in her antechamber. Nothing, again, pleased her more than to win some proselyte from another creed, or to reclaim some repentant prodigal of the Court; and Saint Simon tells us how easily she was imposed upon by one Courcillon, whom she nursed through an illness, and to whom she would talk and read good books for hours at a time, though when she left the room this impudent young libertine would take her off for the benefit of his friends, and send them into fits of laughter by his clever imitation. But then, adds Saint Simon, "Madame de Maintenon was always the queen of dupes."

Her own room, with its crucifixes and books of devotion and sacred pictures, was more like an oratory than a boudoir, and Versailles generally took a tone of gravity and sobriety that must have contrasted strangely with the dissipation of former days. Louis himself observed all the fasts and festivals of the Church, attended Mass, and received the Sacrament with the ardour of a new convert; and the courtiers followed his Majesty to chapel, and watched him at his prayers, with the same regularity that they attended his *levée* or his promenade. "Racine has surpassed himself," wrote Madame de Sévigné; "he loves his God as he used to love his mistresses."

As may be supposed, this outward devotion was often the merest pretence, and those who attended Mass the most regularly were in many instances the most dissolute courtiers. "The profession of a hypocrite," wrote Molière, "had marvellous advantages;" and a more detestable form of hypocrisy cannot well be conceived than that impersonated in "Tartuffe," or in "Onuphre," one of the characters of La Bruyère. Saint Simon tells us story after story to show how false and hollow the fashionable religion was in reality: the two gay old ladies who relieved their consciences by making their servants fast; Orleans reading a black-covered volume at Mass, with an appearance of great devotion, but which proved to be Rabelais instead of a breviary; Madame de Maintenon's bosom friend, the Princess of Harcourt, discovered playing cards when she ought to have been at Vespers; Madame de Roncy, who communicated every week, "but had the most evil tongue" at Court; M. d'O, "who had such an air of sanctity and such austerity of manners that one was tempted to cut his cloak in pieces from behind" (*i.e.*, make phylacteries of it). But none of his stories is more characteristic of the time than the practical joke played by Brissac upon these zealous frequenters of the royal chapel.

"Brissac, Captain of the Guard, was an honest fellow, who could not endure what was false. He had seen with impatience all the seats in the chapel lined with ladies at evening service on Thursdays and Sundays during the winter, because they knew the king never missed attending himself; but if they knew early enough that the king was not coming, not a soul was to be seen there. On the pretence of reading their breviaries, they all had little candlesticks in front of them, so as to let their faces be seen and recognised.

"One evening, when the king was expected to come to service, and the usual preliminary prayer had been read, and the Guards were at their posts, and the ladies all arranged in their places, Brissac comes in, just as the prayer is over, raises his baton, and gives his orders in a loud voice: 'Gentlemen of the Royal Guard, retire and withdraw to your quarters; his Majesty is not coming this evening.'

"As soon as the Guards had obeyed, there was whispering among the ladies in a low tone; the little candles were extinguished; and off they all went except Madame de Dangeau and a few others, who remained. Brissac had placed officers at some of the doorways leading from the chapel, who ordered the Guards to take up their posts again, as soon as the ladies were far enough off for there to be no doubt of their departure.

"Presently the king arrived, and, greatly astonished at seeing no ladies in the galleries, he inquired how it happened there was no one there. As they were leaving the chapel, Brissac told him what he had done, and expatiated on the piety of the ladies of the Court. The king laughed heartily at the trick, and so did all those with him. The story soon got about, and all the ladies would have liked to have strangled Brissac."

Again, if the following anecdote is true, this mock devotion was often accompanied by an ignorance worthy of the dark ages of Christianity. Count Grammont was one of the greatest wits and finest gentlemen of his day.

"Being seriously ill at the age of eighty-four, a year before his death, his wife spoke to him of God. The utter forgetfulness in which he had lived all his life threw him into a strange sort of surprise at the mysteries revealed to him. At last, turning to her—'But now, Countess,' he asked, 'are you telling me the very truth?' Then, hearing her read the Lord's Prayer,—'Countess,' said he again to her, 'this prayer is beautiful. Who composed it?' He had not the least particle of any religion."

The Jesuits, by all accounts, seem to have been responsible for much of this inconsistency between profession and practice. With them religion took its most attractive form, and could be associated with all that made life pleasant—with wine and love, with gay dresses and sumptuous living. Falsehood, murder, and adultery were no longer the deadly sins that had been supposed; pardon could be obtained, and indulgences might be bought, if recourse was had to a Jesuit confessor. With a Jesuit at hand, the most hardened sinner had no occasion to despair—"for," says Saint Simon, "they deceive him, from motives of worldly policy, up to the brink of the tomb, and conduct him to it in profound peace along a path strewn with flowers."

"Masters of the Court, through their position as confessors to nearly all the kings and catholic sovereigns; masters of almost every state through their instruction of youth, their talents, and their diplomacy; necessary to Rome, in order to insinuate her pretensions over the temporal power of sovereigns, and her supremacy over all things spiritual, so as to annihilate the episcopate and general councils; formidable from their power and their wealth, entirely devoted to the purposes of their Order; carrying authority by their multifarious knowledge, and by every art of insinuation; winning men's affections by an easiness and a tact (*tour*) which had never yet been met with at the confessional, and protected by Rome as being especially devoted to the Pope by a fourth vow, peculiar to their society, and more peculiarly fitted than any other class to extend his supreme dominion; in other respects, recommending themselves by the austerity of a life entirely consecrated to study and the defence of the Church against heretics, as well as by the sanctity of their early Fathers; lastly, terrible by a policy the most refined and the most profound, which postponed every other earthly consideration to that of power, and sustained by an internal government in which absolute authority, subordination of rank, secrecy, expediency, uniformity in views, and multiplicity of means—were the inspiring principles."

It was not long, says Saint Simon, before Madame de Maintenon's religious zeal began to take a more active form. She persuaded the king that the conversion of the Protestants would put the coping-stone on the glories of his reign,—that he might thus vindicate his title of Most Christian Majesty, and prove a second Theodosius or Constantine. After various enactments increasing in severity, the famous Edict of Nantes, by which Henry IV. had insured safety and toleration to his Protestant subjects, was formally revoked in 1693; and then began that persecution "which was not to cost a drop of blood," and which was made infamous by what were known in history as "the Dragonnades of Louvois."

"This frightful plot," says Saint Simon, " depopulated a quarter of the kingdom, ruined its commerce, enfeebled it in every part, gave it up for years to the open and avowed pillage of the soldiery, authorised torments and punishments in which many innocent persons of both sexes died in reality by thousands, ruined a host of people, tore asunder a world of families, armed relations against relations, to seize their goods and leave them to die of hunger, made our manufactures pass to strangers, and caused their commonwealths to flourish and overflow at the expense of ours."[1]

Père la Chaise had been the king's confessor for more than thirty years, and Saint Simon speaks warmly of his gentle and liberal character. All his influence—so far as it could be exercised—seems to have been for good. He befriended Fénelon in his exile; he did his best to shelter the fugitives of Port Royal; and he scandalised his orthodox friends by keeping on his table a copy of a Jansenist commentary on the Gospels, explaining that he liked good wherever he found it. Feeling the infirmities of age creeping on him (for he was now more than eighty), the old man had several times petitioned to be allowed to give up his duties; but Louis would not hear of it, and to the last Père la Chaise continued to absolve his royal penitent, though his own memory had failed, and his mind wandered. Shortly before his

[1] These barbarities do not seem to have offended the public opinion of the day, for we find Madame de Sévigné writing in the pleasantest way possible from her country-house in Brittany: "Oh no, we are not so dull here. Hanging is our amusement just now. They have just taken twenty or thirty of these fellows, and are going to throw them off." And again, she says her son-in-law has "just made a fatiguing journey to pursue and punish these wretched Huguenots, who came forth from their holes, and vanished like ghosts to avoid extermination."

death, he asked the king as a special favour to choose his successor from among the Jesuits,—hinting that unless he did so, "a dangerous blow might be struck, and it would not be for the first time." Louis, says Saint Simon, "wanted to live," and therefore took good care to choose his new confessor from the Order of Jesus. He selected Père Tellier—the very opposite in mind, manner, and body, of the good, easy Père la Chaise—a kind of arch-Jesuit, regarded with terror even by his own brethren, and with something like horror by Saint Simon, although from the first Tellier made him friendly advances, and, as we shall see, asked his advice and opinion as to the celebrated "Constitution."

"The first time that Père Tellier saw the king in his cabinet after having been presented to him, there were only present Bloin (the valet) and Fagon (the doctor) in a corner. Fagon, bent double, and leaning on his staff, watched the interview closely, as well as the countenance of this new personage, with his bowings and scrapings and his answers. The king asked him if he was a relation of Messieurs Le Tellier (the Chancellor and the Bishop). The good Father bowed himself to the dust. 'I, sire,' answered he, 'a relative of Messieurs Le Tellier! *I* am very far from being that; I am a poor peasant from Lower Normandy, where my father was a farmer.' Fagon, who had watched him closely, so as not to lose a word, twisted himself up, and made an effort to look at Bloin. 'Sir,' said he, pointing to the Jesuit, 'what a cursed scoundrel!' and shrugging his shoulders, leant again upon his staff."

Saint Simon says he was not far wrong; indeed Père Tellier, as Saint Simon describes him, is almost the ideal Jesuit of fiction. Harsh, exacting, laborious—

"With a heart and brain of iron, and an enemy of all amusement and dissipation;" false and unscrupulous, with "his real character hid under a thousand folds, and owning no god but the interests of the Order. . . . He would have been a terrible fellow to have met in a dark lane, with his cloudy, false, and sinister countenance, and his eyes burning with an evil radiance, and squinting in both directions."

To his ascendancy over the mind of Louis, Saint Simon attributes the persecution of the Jansenists, whose doctrines seem to have been a milder form of Calvinism. Jansen's 'Augustinus' (which contained the famous "Five Propositions" condemned by the Pope) insisted much on the efficacy and necessity of divine grace, vouchsafed only to a few, and obtained only by continual prayer. Generally speaking, it was a protest and reaction against the insincerity of the religion of the day, and the dangerous morality of the Jesuits. Jansen and his followers denounced, both in precept and in practice, the whole of that gorgeous ritual by which the Church of Rome seeks to make her creed attractive and imposing. The music and the incense, the paintings and the images, the embroidery and the vestments, were all proscribed. When the Jansenist worshipped, the service was to be in the simplest and severest style; the Gospel was to be read in the vulgar tongue, the Psalms were to be chanted, and hymns might be sung, but there was to be no "ritual," no High Mass, and no frequent celebration of the Sacrament. It was by prayer, by solitude, by fasting, by suffering, by humiliation, by all that could mortify both soul and body, that man could alone hope to draw near his Maker.

So much of what the Jansenists professed and taught seems clear, but notwithstanding, half the world in those days appears never to have agreed or understood what was exactly implied in Jansenism.[1] According to Saint Simon, the Jesuits "invented this heresy, which had neither founders nor followers," to serve their own purpose; and then induced Louis, who had always associated Port Royal with the Fronde, to believe Jansenism to be synonymous with treason and impiety, and to regard a Jansenist as the avowed enemy of social order. That this was Louis's actual impression may be gathered from the following story, which Saint Simon has told us twice over:—

"Among those whom the Duke of Orleans wished to be of his suite in his journey [to Spain in 1708], he named Fontpertuis. At this name the king at once put on a severe air.

"'How is this, nephew? Fontpertuis, the son of that Jansenist—that silly woman who ran everywhere after M. Arnauld! I could not think of allowing a man of that sort to go with you.'

"'By my faith, Sire,' answered the Duke, 'I don't know what the mother has done! but as for the son, *he* has taken good care not to be a Jansenist, I will answer for that, for he does not even believe in God.'

"'Is it possible?' replied the king, recovering his good-humour.

"'Nothing more certain, Sire, I can assure you,' replied the Duke.

---

[1] Even now, many orthodox Catholics suppose that the Jansenists were Socinians, Calvinists, bastard Lutherans; and one writer couples Jansen with Mahomet, and boldly pronounces a Jansenist to be "a worshipper of Satan"—Histoire universelle de l'Eglise catholique, xiii. 295.

"'Since that is so,' said the king, 'there is no harm in him. You may take him with you.'

"This scene (for one can call it by no other name) took place in the morning, and the Duke of Orleans told it me after dinner the same day, almost dying with laughter, word for word, just as I have written it down. After we had both of us laughed heartily at it, we admired the profound learning of a devout and religious king."

The story went the round of the Court, and every one laughed at it,—although, says Saint Simon, some of the more thoughtful courtiers were more inclined to weep than laugh over such ignorance, coupled with such bigotry, in the person of "his Most Christian Majesty."

Rightly or wrongly, Port Royal had been always regarded as the headquarters of Jansenism, and the Jesuits had determined on its destruction. The story of these "solitary and illustrious saints" (to use Saint Simon's words)—of Arnauld and Le Maistre, of Saint Cyran and La Mère Angélique, of Pascal and the famous "Letters," in which he appealed to the world against the dogmatists of his day—of the closing of the monastery and the dispersion of the recluses,—all this has been fully told in another volume of this series.[1]

Of Port Royal itself, in 1701, nothing was left but a ruined chapel and graveyard, and a convent where twenty-two aged nuns still lingered on, whom Louis himself would willingly have left alone to die there in peace. His surgeon, Maréchal, had been deeply impressed by the patience and piety of these holy women, and his report had strongly influenced his master. But the terrible Père Tellier had resolved on their disper-

---

[1] "Pascal," by Principal Tulloch.

sion. Feeling their case was hopeless with the Jesuits against them, the unfortunate nuns appealed to Rome, but the Pope only responded by a bull which ordered that "this nest of heresy should be uprooted from its foundations," and the Cardinal de Noailles had no alternative but to enforce the papal mandate.

In the autumn of 1709 Port Royal was surrounded by a body of archers under Argenson, lieutenant of the police; the nuns were summoned to the chapter-house; the royal commission was read to them, and then they were hurried into carriages, and each of them carried off to a different convent. The parting scene between these aged sisters, many of them sick and infirm—their tears, their misery, their agonising farewells—moved even the rough archers of the Guard to pity.

But even this dispersion of the nuns did not satisfy the Jesuits. There still remained the graveyard—"the necropolis of Jansenism"—where the ashes of three thousand recluses of Port Royal reposed in what might have been thought consecrated ground. It was ordered that the bodies should be exhumed, and the graveyard ploughed up, and a gang of workmen were sent down for the purpose. For two months they continued their odious task, and their horrible profanity excited the deepest resentment among the relatives and descendants of those whose graves were thus shamefully violated. After the bodies had been removed, the plough was passed over the burial-ground, and the church and cloisters were destroyed so completely that not one stone was left upon another.

Innocent XII. had died in 1700—"a great and holy Pope," says Saint Simon; "a true pastor and common father of the Church, such as one rarely sees in Saint

Peter's chair." He was succeeded by Clement XI., as weak as he was amiable, who gave way to the pressure brought to bear on him by the Jesuits. After various refusals and delays, he at length published the celebrated bull *Unigenitus*, which condemned a hundred and one propositions contained in Père Quesnil's commentary on the Gospels, which, on its first appearance, some thirty years previously, had been quoted and admired by orthodox Catholics.[1] The " Constitution," as the bull was called, was received both at Rome and in France with indignation and alarm " by all," says Saint Simon, " excepting those who were enslaved to the Jesuits— that is to say, by honest people in every class of life." The cardinals protested against it; many of the bishops refused to recognise it; the doctors of the Sorbonne denounced its terms; and though the Parliament ratified it, as being " by order of the king," it was with sullen murmurs of disapproval. Every one wondered how the Pope could have been induced to pass such a sweeping sentence of condemnation on recognised authorities, and this is the explanation that Saint Simon had from Amelot, who had been sent as a special envoy to Rome on this occasion:—

"He told me that the Pope had taken a liking to him, and often spoke to him in confidence, groaning over the straits in which he found himself, and over his powerlessness to do as he pleased. In one of these conversations the Pope opened his heart on his regret at having ever allowed himself to publish the " Constitution;" that it was the king's letters that had extracted it from him, and those of Père Tellier;

---

[1] See p. 104.

... **and** that if he had expected a hundredth part of the opposition he had met with, he would never have given his consent to the measure.

"Thereupon, Amelot frankly asked him why, if this was so, and he wanted to publish a bull at all, he had not contented himself with censuring a few of the propositions in Père Quesnel's book, instead of making a clean sweep of a hundred and one propositions. Then the Pope cried out and began to weep, and, seizing him by the arm, said thus in Italian: 'Ah, Monsieur Amelot, Monsieur Amelot! what would you have had me do? I fought inch by inch to get rid of some of them; but Père Tellier had told the king that there was in this book more than a hundred propositions deserving censure; he did not wish to pass for a liar, and his party held me down by the throat until they made me condemn more than a hundred, to show that he had spoken the truth, *and I have only put one more in the bull!* See, see, Monsieur Amelot! how could I have acted otherwise?'"

Whether this pitiable confession of weakness on the part of Clement XI. is true or not, there is no doubt as to the pressure put upon him by the Jesuits, nor as to the persecution employed to enforce submission to the "Constitution." All who refused to agree to its clauses were "*tenus pour suspects*," and, as before, hundreds of innocent persons were imprisoned or sent into exile. No class felt safe from attack when such men as Rollin, Fontenelle, and La Chapelle were arrested by the police. Poor students of theology, inoffensive merchants, sisters of charity, were among the first victims. Even at Versailles the sense of insecurity was so general, that Madame de Saint Simon warned her husband not to talk too loudly about the "Constitution," or he would inevitably find himself in the Bastille.

The Jesuits were triumphant for the time, and Père

Tellier found means to reward such of his satellites as had been most active in procuring this condemnation of Jansenism, and thereby advancing " the greater glory of God," as well as of their Order. A pension was given to Lerouge; Rohan and Polignac each received a rich preferment, and Bissy got a cardinal's hat. It was even proposed to establish the Inquisition in France; and one Jesuit (Lallemand) enlarged on its merits to the Marshal d'Estrées. " The Marshal," says Saint Simon, "let him talk on a little while, and then, the fire mounting to his face, he cut him short by telling him that, if it was not out of respect for the house where they were (the Abbey of Saint Germain du Pré), he would have thrown him out of the window." Fifteen years afterwards, in 1732, another Jesuit (P. du Halde) made a similar proposal to Saint Simon. "I took him up," he says, "in such a rough fashion, that all his life afterwards he never dared to speak of it again to me."

The Protestants did not escape a second persecution, any more than the Jansenists. In 1712 a new edict was passed against them. Those who would not conform to the Catholic faith were no longer allowed to practise their simple worship in caves and desert places as heretofore, but were pursued and apprehended by the police and soldiers. The men were sent to the galleys; the women were imprisoned; and their pastors, if they were found officiating, were hung in chains by the roadside. The tale of their wrongs and sufferings has been so often and so pathetically told, that there is no need for dwelling upon it here. It is the blackest spot in the history of the time, and Saint Simon's indignant denunciation of the authors and instigators of this barbarous policy is only a faint echo of the deep and passionate resentment that it roused both in Paris and the provinces. One has only to turn to the caricatures and pasquinades of the day to find abundant proofs that in this respect he has not exaggerated the intensity of popular feeling. Whether he is right in ascribing this policy, as he does, to the sinister influence of Madame de Maintenon, is another question. After all, he says, she was herself "the dupe of her own hypocrisy," and a mere puppet in the hands of the Jesuits.

"She believed herself the prophetess who should save the people of God from error, from revolt, and from impiety. It was in this belief, with which Bissy[1] inspired her, that she excited the king to all the horrors, all the violences, all the acts of tyranny then practised upon men's consciences, upon their fortunes and their persons, and which filled the prisons and dungeons. Bissy suggested and obtained all he wished.

. . . .

"The barbarous measures taken with the Huguenots after the revocation of the Edict of Nantes were on a large scale the model of those now taken with all who would not agree to the 'Constitution.' Hence arose the innumerable artifices used to intimidate and gain over the bishops, the schools, and the lower clergy; hence came that vast and ceaseless storm of *lettres de cachet*, that struggle with the Parliament, that total denial of public and private justice, that open inquisition and persecution even reaching to simple laymen —a whole people exiled or shut up in prisons; and lastly, the inexhaustible devils' broth (*pot au noir*), to besmear all whom the Jesuits would, . . . and that countless throng of persons of every age and every sex exposed to the same trials of faith as those endured by the Christians under the Arian emperors, and, above all, under Julian the Apostate."

---

[1] Bissy succeeded Bossuet as Bishop of Meaux.

It is curious, after reading this tirade, to find Saint Simon in another passage complacently saying that he had always been on good terms with the Jesuits, and was looked upon by them as a friend and supporter of their interests. But the fact is, that he was himself oppressed and almost terrified by the illimitable power of the Jesuits in that age; and, so far as it was possible in him to play the courtier, he certainly paid court to what he felt to be the strongest body in the kingdom. Yet, while he was ostensibly Père Tellier's excellent friend, —while he even opposed the proposition of his colleague Noailles to expel the Jesuits "bag and baggage" from France—he has not scrupled to describe, in the strongest language at his command, the deadly tendencies of their doctrines; and at one of his secret interviews with Père Tellier, he plainly denounced some of the clauses of the bull *Unigenitus* as revolutionary, and dangerous to the very existence of a monarchy.

"This short statement of mine exasperated the Jesuit, because it hit the right nail on the head, in spite of all his cavilling and equivocation. All the time he avoided saying anything personally offensive, but he fumed with rage, and . . . in his furious passion, being no longer master of himself, many things escaped him which I feel sure he would afterwards have paid very dearly to have left in silence. He told me so much of the extremities and the violence that would be used to make the 'Constitution' accepted—things so enormous, so atrocious, so frightful, and all with such furious passion—that I fell into a veritable syncope. I saw him face to face between two candles, there being only the breadth of the table between us—(I have described elsewhere his horrible countenance)—and all at once, stupefied both in sight and hearing, I comprehended, while he was speaking, all that was implied in a Jesuit,—a man who, by his personal annihilation, and bound by the vows of his Order, could hope for nothing for his family or for himself—not even an apple or a glass of water more than his brethren,—who was so old as to be even then drawing near the time when he must give an account to God, and yet with deliberate purpose, and with studied artifice, was about to throw State and Church into the most terrific conflagration, and begin the most frightful persecution for questions that mattered not a jot to him, nor touched in any degree the honour of the school of Molina.

"His deep and dark designs, and the violence that he showed, so bewildered and confounded me, that I suddenly interrupted him and said, 'My father, how old are you?' The extreme surprise (for I was looking at him with all my eyes) that I saw painted on his face recalled me to my senses, and his answer completely restored me to myself. 'Eh! why do you ask me that?' said he, smiling. The effort that I made to avoid this fearful dilemma, of which I felt all the terrible importance, furnished me with a way of escape. 'It is because,' said I, 'I have never looked at you so long as I have now, face to face and between these two candles, and you have such a fine healthy countenance, with all your labours, that I am perfectly surprised at it.'

"He swallowed the answer—or at least made such a good pretence of doing so, that he said nothing of it at the time or since, and never ceased to speak to me as often as he had done before, and with the same openness, although I sought his company less than ever. He told me that he was seventy-four years of age; that, as a matter of fact, he was in excellent health, and had accustomed himself to toil and hardship all his life. And then he took up the conversation again at the point where I had interrupted him."

Saint Simon's own religious views (although he is not always consistent in the matter) are pretty much what we might expect from his shrewd yet earnest character.

He tells us frankly that he was himself "*ni docte ni docteur;*" that he had neither the time nor inclination to trouble himself about vexed questions of theology; that he had put himself in the hands of La Trappe, his spiritual adviser; and that La Trappe had warned him that Jansenism was a deadly heresy,—that there was neither charity, nor peace, nor truth in its tenets, and that it was dangerous alike to Church and State.

But if he was not a Jansenist, still less was he a Jesuit or an Ultramontane. He was warmly attached to the Gallican Church, and thought it had done good service in defending its liberties against the "aggressions and usurpations of the Court of Rome." He recognised in the Pope "the chief of the Church, the successor of Saint Peter, the first bishop, but very far from being infallible, *in whatever sense one takes the words.*" In fact, his view of the papal supremacy is that of a moderate Catholic but not of an Ultramontane; and it is clear that anything like bigotry or intolerance, especially in the form of persecution, was abhorrent to his whole nature.

He passed a week or more every Easter at the monastery of La Trappe, only a few miles from his own country-house. The Abbot had been a distinguished soldier in the Fronde, but had retired from the world (it was said from disappointed love), and had for some thirty years led a life of penance and seclusion that seemed to have reached the limits of asceticism. Saint Simon always speaks of him with the profoundest veneration, and his affection was evidently returned. "He loved me as a father," he says, "and I loved him as a son."

So attached was he to the Abbot of La Trappe, and

so anxious to have some memorial of him, that he got Rigault to paint his portrait from memory, and the likeness was pronounced admirable. The fact of the picture having been taken at all was to have been kept a profound secret, but Rigault could not resist the temptation of making money by painting copies of it, and Saint Simon had to confess the trick he had played upon his confessor. La Trappe was much vexed, though he forgave the culprit. "I hate treason, but I love the traitor," was his way of condoning the offence. When he died, Saint Simon's grief was intense. "These Memoirs," he says, "are too profane to recall anything here of a life so sublimely holy, and of a death so grand and so precious in the sight of God. . . . All Europe felt his loss acutely; the Church wept for him; and even the world did him justice."

Next to La Trappe, Saint Simon had more sympathy perhaps with Fénelon than with any other prelate of the day, although he has discovered a strain of worldliness in Fénelon's character which his other biographers have passed over or ignored. His piety, he says, was "of that insinuating kind which is all things to all men:" his ambition had led him "to knock at all doors," and to pass from the Jesuits over to the Jansenists; but being "too subtle" (*trop fin*) for the latter, he had halted half-way with the Sulpicians, and made himself a reputation for his "penetrating genius" and courtly manners. Then Bossuet had taken him up; Beauvilliers was fascinated by him; he was appointed tutor to the young Duke of Burgundy, and all would have gone well with him at Court had he not, in an evil hour for himself, made Madame Guyon's acquaintance. Fénelon, whose imagination was easily touched, was charmed with this young prophetess. "Their spirituality amalgamated," says Saint Simon. He introduced her at Versailles, and Madame de Maintenon herself was among the distinguished converts attracted by this new phase of mysticism. Delightful little dinner-parties took place, when the guests interchanged spiritual confidences, and all "with a secrecy and mystery that gave additional flavour to this precious manna." Madame Guyon even made her way into Saint Cyr, and the young girls there (as may be supposed) eagerly welcomed anything that relieved the monotony of their lives; indeed, they seem to have occasionally dreamed dreams and seen visions when they ought to have been engaged in their studies or household work.

Unfortunately both for Fénelon and Madame Guyon, Godet, the Bishop of Chartres—a stern divine, who had little sympathy with enthusiasm in any shape—discovered the dangerous tendencies of these new doctrines; and Bossuet, whom he consulted, took the same view. Madame de Maintenon was startled and indignant to find that "she had been led to the verge of a precipice," and at once repudiated her friends. Madame Guyon was banished from Saint Cyr, and soon afterwards sent to the Bastille.

Fénelon, who to the last regarded this enthusiast as a persecuted saint, wished apparently to justify both her and himself, if it was possible, and wrote a book on the history of mysticism, called 'Maxims of the Saints.' This book, according to Saint Simon, was quite unintelligible "except to the Masters of Israel;" and those theologians who could understand it agreed that it was "pure and refined Quietism, disguised under a barbarous language." Its publication only increased the prejudice against Fénelon at Court; and Bossuet soon afterwards wrote two volumes in reply—" clear, short, concise, and supported by countless references from Holy Scripture, the Fathers, and the Councils;" and we are told that it was " received and devoured with avidity."

Fénelon's book was condemned by a commission of bishops. He was banished from Court to his diocese; Louis with his own hand crossed his name off the list of the royal household, and all who knew the king knew that, while he lived, the sentence was irrevocable. Almost immediately afterwards his book was placed by the Pope on the *Index Expurgatorius;* and whoever was found reading it, or even having it in his possession, was threatened with excommunication. The news of this last blow reached Fénelon just as he was mounting the pulpit in his church at Cambray. He at once laid aside his prepared sermon, and preached extempore on the duty of submission to the powers that be. He had still influential supporters among the Jesuits, and his friends hoped that such prompt obedience might have made his peace both with the king and the Pope. But this was not to be.

" Confined within his diocese, this prelate grew old there under the useless burden of his hopes, and saw the years glide by with a sameness (*égalité*) that could not but make him despair. Always hateful to the king, to whom no one dared mention his name even on indifferent subjects—more hateful still to Madame de Maintenon because she had ruined him—more exposed than any other to that terrible cabal which ruled over Monseigneur—he had no resource except in the unchangeable affection of his pupil [the Duke of Burgundy], himself a victim of this cabal. . . . Then in the twinkling of an eye the pupil becomes the Dauphin, and in another moment, as one will see, he is raised to a kind of viceroyalty (*avant-règne*). What a change of fortune for a man of Fénelon's ambitious character!"

Saint Simon dwells at some length, and in more than one passage, upon Fénelon's peaceful and laborious life in his diocese, his charity to the poor, his visits to the hospitals, his grand hospitality, his kindness to the clergy, his urbanity and courtly manners; but he hints that, though occupied by his pastoral duties, and though delighting in his books and his flowers—the best companions of solitude—he still cast a longing eye to Versailles, to his young "Telemachus," and to the little band of friends, such as Beauvilliers and Chevreuse, who had never forgotten him during the twelve years of his exile. They still corresponded with him incessantly, and made him the confidant of their hopes and schemes for the future. They received his advice " as though his words were the oracles of God." They never ceased, as they assured him, "to talk of him, to regret him, to long for his return, to cling closer and closer to his memory, as the Jews clung to Jerusalem of old, and to sigh and hope always for his coming again, as that unhappy race still waits for and sighs after the Messiah."

How sadly their hopes were dissipated by the sudden death of the young Dauphin will be told in another chapter. Fénelon and his pupil only lived to meet once again—when the latter was on his way to join the army in Flanders in 1708, and his route lay through Cambray. The prince threw himself upon Fénelon's neck, and if words were wanting, says Saint Simon, "the fire from his looks, darting into the eyes of the archbishop, supplied all that the king had forbidden him to say, and was an eloquence that carried away the spectators." But this was the last and only interview between "Mentor" and "Telemachus."

Fénelon survived the Dauphin some four years, and, "even after so many losses and trials, this prelate was still a man of hopes." Orleans had declared that, if he became Regent, his first step would be to recall him from banishment. But it was too late: Fénelon's health, never strong, had been broken by incessant labour, by grief, and by disappointment. In 1715 he lost his life-long friend, the Duke of Beauvilliers, and this last blow struck him to the heart. A few months later he was himself carried to his last resting-place, dying as he had lived, "a model ever-present that none could attain to; in all things a true prelate; in all things also a grand seigneur, and in all things still more—the author of 'Telemachus.'" Such is his epitaph, as Saint Simon has written it for us; or, as we might put it now, the Christian bishop, the perfect gentleman, and the accomplished scholar. Taking him all in all, we may search ecclesiastical history far and wide before we discover his superior, or even his equal.

CHAPTER IX.

THE SPANISH SUCCESSION.

SAINT SIMON'S warmest admirers must admit that his account of the great war that convulsed Europe in the last decade of Louis XIV.'s reign is partial and unsatisfactory, and it is fortunate, on every ground, that we have not to depend upon his history of the campaigns that followed the accession of Philip V. to the throne of Spain. As it happens, this period is singularly rich in contemporary memoirs. We have the despatches of Marlborough on one side, and of Vendôme and Villars on the other; we have the letters of such masters of the art of war as Berwick and Prince Eugene; and we have the independent opinion of diplomatists like Torcy and De Noailles. When collated with such evidence, Saint Simon is found to be as often wrong as right. His prejudices and personal dislikes are shown in his account of almost every battle; and while he does full justice to the talents of Marlborough, and even pays his tribute to William III., the sworn enemy of his country, he cannot find a good word to say for the gallant French soldiers who were fighting against long odds, dying of hunger in their camps, and perishing by thousands on the fields of Blenheim and Malplaquet.

A civilian is rarely a competent critic of the art of war, and Saint Simon, in spite of his four campaigns, was essentially a politician, and not a soldier. He was only present himself at one battle, and of that battle (Neerwinden) he has given us an amateur's account. He could paint the details that came under his own eye, but failed utterly to grasp the general plan of action. Like a painter who makes his sketch from a particular point of view, he brings some one scene or episode into strong relief, but ignores all that does not actually meet his eye. Again, writing, as he wrote, from his cabinet at Versailles, what could he possibly know of the real circumstances of half of what he tells us? He was not in the confidence of any of the Ministers excepting Chamillart, who soon resigned his office; he rarely saw any of the despatches; he was at deadly feud with most of the generals; there were no bulletins, no "special correspondents," and private letters were few and far between. What he heard was principally the gossip of the backstairs or second-hand reports from second-rate authorities; and we may be sure that he eagerly caught at anything that would glorify his young hero, the Duke of Burgundy, or cast discredit on Villars, or Villeroy, or Vendôme.

As is well known, the grand question of succession, over which so much blood was subsequently spilt, was whether Charles II.'s enormous possessions, "on which the sun never set"—Spain, half the Netherlands, Milan, Sicily, Naples, Mexico, Cuba, and the African colonies—were to go to a French or an Austrian prince, to enrich the house of Bourbon or the house of Hapsburg. More than one secret treaty had been drawn up between the parties chiefly interested in Charles's death, which divided the Spanish possessions between France and Austria,—Louis, of course, getting the lion's share in the division. Unfortunately, Charles heard of the last treaty concluded at the Hague between Louis and William III., and, exasperated at the thought of his kingdom being thus dismembered in his own lifetime, he drew up a fresh will, by which he left the whole of his vast possessions to the Duke of Anjou, the grandson of Louis XIV.

The excitement in Madrid was intense when, shortly afterwards, Charles died, and it was known that he had made a new will,—for public opinion in Madrid was divided between the Bourbons and the house of Hapsburg. The Council of State assembled at the palace, and the antechambers were thronged by nobles, Spanish dignitaries, and by foreign ambassadors, each eager to hear the terms of the will, and to inform their Court. Among the rest stood Blécourt the French ambassador, and Harrach the Austrian envoy, the latter being posted close to the door, with an eager and triumphant air.

"At length the door opened and closed again. The Duc d'Abrantes, who was a man with plenty of wit and a dangerous kind of humour, wished to have the pleasure of announcing the successor to the throne, as soon as he had seen the council agreed. He found himself surrounded the moment he showed himself outside. He cast his eye round him on all sides, still gravely keeping silence. Blécourt advanced. D'Abrantes looked at him very intently, and then turning his head the other way, seemed as though he were seeking for what he had almost in front of him,—an action which surprised Blécourt, and made him interpret it as of evil augury for France. Then suddenly making as though he had only just perceived the Count d'Harrach for the first time, D'Abrantes put on an air of joy, threw himself on his neck, and said to him in Spanish in a loud tone: 'Sir, it is with the greatest pleasure'—and making a pause in order to embrace him better, he went on—'Yes, sir, it is with extreme joy that for the whole of my life'—and then redoubling his embrace, to give himself an excuse for stopping once more, he finished with—'and with the greatest satisfaction, that I separate myself from you, and take my leave of the most august house of Austria.' And then he made his way through the crowd, every one running after him to know the name of the real heir. The astonishment and indignation of D'Harrach closed his mouth altogether, but showed themselves through his face."

It was not likely that Philip V.'s accession would be tamely acquiesced in by the members of the Grand Alliance, and the emperor declared war at once against France; but public opinion was divided in England, and for the present that country made no sign. But, in 1701, James II. died at St Germains, and, whether out of generosity or bravado, or to gratify his hatred against William III., Louis publicly recognised the heir of the Stuarts as the King of England. "It was a stupidity," says Saint Simon, "of which a child would not have been guilty." By this folly he turned the English nation into a personal enemy, and England threw herself heart and soul into the war which followed, supplying, in proportion to her size, more men and money than any other of the allied powers.

Soon after this, William, who had been long in declining health, met with the accident which gave the last blow to his shattered constitution. He died—"but his spirit still continued to animate the Grand Alliance, and his bosom friend Heinsius perpetuated it, and inspired with it all the chiefs of the Republic, their allies and generals, in such a fashion, that it was scarcely apparent that William was no more." France had against her the two greatest generals of the age—Eugene of Savoy, and Marlborough himself, who, says Voltaire, "was more of a king than William, as great a statesman, and a far greater general."

Meanwhile, calamities seemed to thicken around France. The campaigns that followed 1702 were a succession of blunders and disasters, culminating in the crushing defeat at Blenheim, or Hochstedt, as the French prefer to call it, where Tallard allowed his army to be cut in half, and where 11,000 men, who had been cooped up within the walls of the village, laid down their arms without striking a blow. Out of the army of 60,000 men that had paraded on the morning of Blenheim, scarcely 5000 answered the muster-roll when Marsin joined Villeroy a few days after the battle.

The news reached Versailles when it was ablaze with illuminations in honour of the birth of a young prince; but the details only transpired by degrees. That there had been a great defeat was well known, but the extent of the calamity could not even be guessed at. Neither despatches nor private letters threw any light on the national disaster, for the simple reason that no one dared to tell the truth. At last, an officer who had been taken prisoner was dismissed on parole by Marlborough to bring the news to Marly, "and," says Saint Simon, "one can imagine what was the general consternation, when each noble family (without speaking of others) had its dead, its wounded, and its prisoners. We trembled in the midst of Alsace."

Next year Marlborough defeated Villeroy at Ramillies, where the battle was decided in half an hour; the French lost six thousand men, and all their guns and baggage, while the whole of Flanders lay open to the victorious army. Here again Saint Simon attributes the defeat entirely to the deplorable blunders of Villeroy, who had posted his raw recruits in the centre, had isolated his left wing behind a marsh, and had actually placed the baggage-waggons between his front line and the reserves.

Vendôme gained some successes in Spain, but these were soon neutralised by the disastrous battle of Turin, which, says Saint Simon, "cost us all Italy, owing to the ambition of La Feuillade, the incapacity of Marsin, the avarice, the trickery, the disobedience of the captains opposed to the Duke of Orleans."

In 1708 Vendôme again took the field in Flanders, but, by a fatal policy, the Duke of Burgundy was associated with him in the command; and this young prince, with all his amiable qualities, had no pretension to any military talent. Even by Saint Simon's account, he seems to have divided his time between hearing Mass, playing tennis, and dawdling over mechanical experiments. "You will win the kingdom of heaven, Monseigneur," said Gamaches, one of his suite; "but as for the kingdom of earth, Eugene and Marlborough take more trouble about getting it than you do." The enemy was not slow to profit by the division of counsel in the French camp, and their forces were concentrated upon Oudenarde, where a disastrous battle was followed by an even more disastrous retreat. Saint Hilaire was present at the battle, and tells us how stubbornly the French Guardsmen held their ground—how Vendôme himself seized a pike and charged at the head of his grenadiers—and how the household brigade fought like lions to retrieve the day—while fifty battalions under the Duke of Burgundy were watching the battle at a prudent distance. Saint Simon tells us nothing of all this, but says, that when a retreat was proposed at the council of war held after the battle, Vendôme, "pushed as he was to extremities, with rage on his face, and fury in his heart," taunted the young prince with his cowardice, —an enormous insult, says Saint Simon; but it must be confessed that our sympathies are rather with the soldier who fought than with the pious and pedantic Duke of Burgundy, who looked on; and Vendôme might have pleaded in excuse of his rough speech, like Hotspur, that it angered him

"To be so pestered with a popinjay."

It is clear that the feeling at Court ran strongly in Vendôme's favour, for Saint Simon complains that on his return he was almost worshipped "as the hero and tutelary genius of France," while for Burgundy there was nothing but cold looks and a disdainful silence, even from his own family. However, if we may trust our chronicler, Vendôme lost favour as rapidly as he gained it, and, thanks to the persevering hostility of the young Duchess of Burgundy, was banished from Versailles and Marly, and at last from Meudon,—"a triumph equally great in the sight of gods and men."

Not long afterwards, Lille—the strongest fortress in

France—succumbed to Eugene after a heroic resistance, in which we are told the garrison had been reduced to "eat eight hundred horses," and had repelled assault after assault.

"The agitation at Court was extreme, even to indecency. The expectation of a decisive battle engrossed us all. The happy junction of the two armies [under Vendôme and Berwick] was regarded as a certain presage of success. Each delay increased our impatience; every one was restless and uneasy; the king even demanded news from the courtiers, and could not imagine what kept the couriers back. The princes and the suite of all the noblemen and people of the Court were with the army. Every one at Versailles felt the danger of their friends and kinsmen; and the oldest established families saw their fortunes in suspense. For forty hours prayers were offered everywhere; the Duchess of Burgundy passed the night in the chapel, while people believed her in bed, and distracted her ladies by her vigils; and, following her example, all the wives who had husbands in the army never stirred from the churches. Games, and even conversation, had ceased. Fear was painted on every countenance and in every speech in a shameful manner. If a horse passed by a little quickly, every one rushed to the windows without knowing why. Chamillart's rooms were crowded with lackeys, even to the street door, for every one wished to be informed the moment a courier arrived; and this agonising suspense lasted a month, until a battle put an end to our uncertainty. Paris, being further from the source of news, was still more troubled, and the provinces to an even greater extent. The king had written to the bishops to offer up public prayers in terms proportioned to the danger."

It would perhaps be going too far to say that Saint Simon rejoiced in the misfortunes of France; but it is certain that he passes very slightly over the French victories, such as Denain, Almanza, and Villa Viciosa, while he devotes chapter after chapter to the long story of French defeats and disasters. An officer who resigns his commission at the beginning of a war, as in his case, is scarcely in a position to malign and disparage the efforts of men who are giving their life-blood for their country; and it is impossible not to feel something like contempt, when we find Saint Simon dangling about the ante-rooms at Versailles, and fulfilling his self-imposed mission of spy and reporter, while battles were being daily lost and won, and while every prince and noble of military age were taking their share of active service on the frontiers. As he tells us himself, there was scarcely a family about the Court that had not its tale of dead and wounded; yet their intense anxiety for news from the seat of war seems to him "indecent;" he can only show his patriotic interest in the campaigns by betting on the capture of the most important French fortress; and, sitting at home at his ease, he can find no word of generous sympathy for the poor, half-starved, half-clothed soldiers, dragged from their homes, "to die like flies," as Louville said, by famine and sickness, as well as by the sword.

The continued disasters in the war, added to the terribly severe winter of 1709, induced Louis to make overtures of peace, and Torcy was sent on a secret mission to the Hague. The French king only stipulated that Philip should be allowed to keep Naples and Sicily, otherwise he declared himself ready to surrender anything and everything. "But," says St Simon, "his enemies derided his misery, and negotiated only to mock him." Heinsius — the Dutch banker — inspired the allied general with something of the persevering enmity which he had himself inherited from William of Orange; and the demands made by the Allies were so exorbitant that Louis had no alternative but to reject them. " I am a Frenchman as well as a king," he declared, "and what tarnishes the glory of France touches me more closely than my own interests;" and then for the first time in his life he made a personal appeal to his own subjects to rise and repel the invaders. " There was but one cry," says Saint Simon, " of indignation and vengeance; nothing but offers to give all their goods to carry on the war, and to undergo extremities, such as they had undergone before, to mark their zeal." To set an example, Louis sent his gold plate to be melted down, and most of his courtiers imitated their master; and those who could not give money gave themselves.[1] Peasants, mechanics, poor farmers, and broken-down gentlemen, in spite of the misery and distress in the provinces, flocked in numbers to join the ranks, and Louis would have again taken the field in person, had it not been "for the evil genius which held him fast in those domestic fetters, whose weight he never felt." Prayers were offered up in every church throughout the kingdom for the success of the French army, and early in the following spring Villars was sent to try his fortune in Flanders at the head of 110,000 men.

But that year only saw fresh reverses. Tournay, a fortress nearly as strong as Lille, was taken, and the loss was quickly followed by the defeat at Malplaquet,—

---

[1] Saint Simon showed characteristic prudence.—" When I saw that I was almost the only person at Court still eating off silver, I sent a thousand pistoles' worth of it to the Mint, and locked up the rest."

the most obstinate and most murderous battle fought during the war. The victors lost more men than the vanquished, and bivouacked on the field among 25,000 dead. "The Court had grown so accustomed to defeats," says Saint Simon, "that a battle lost, as Malplaquet was, seemed half a victory." Yet he will allow Villars no credit for his own heroic conduct, or for the good order of the retreat. We hear little of the terrible privations endured by the survivors of Malplaquet. "There was no meat or bread; the soldiers ate roots and herbs"— is all that Saint Simon says of the famine that was desolating the camp. Boufflers, we are told, deserved half the glory of the campaign, such as it was; but Boufflers was neglected and disgraced, and died of a broken heart, while Villars received honours and rewards for victories which had been won by his lieutenants. "The name which his invincible good-luck has acquired for him for all future time has often disgusted me with history," says Saint Simon. He was all "*fanfaronnade,*" with "the magnificence of a Gascon, and the greediness of a harpy."

But if Saint Simon is unjust to Villars, he is still more unjust to Vendôme, against whom his hatred breaks out whenever he mentions his name. He ascribes half the misfortunes in the war to his indolence and incapacity, and hints that even his victories were won by his troops, almost in spite of himself. But then Vendôme crossed the arms of France with the bar-sinister; he was closely allied to Monseigneur's faction; he was himself given to wine and riotous living; his home at Anet was Meudon on a grosser scale, or rather an Abbey of Thelema, where all licence was permitted; "his Bohemians," as Saint Simon calls his friends, did nothing but drink and gamble, and rivalled their patron in ribaldry and profanity; and as for his brother, the Grand Prior, we are told that he was "a coward, a liar, a sharper, a scoundrel, and a robber;" that he reverenced nothing on earth except the "divine bottle," and had been carried to bed drunk every night for forty years.

Vendôme's life, no doubt, was scandalous enough, and he had a cynical disdain for the proprieties, and even for the decencies, of society; but of his military talents there can be no question. Even Eugene acknowledged him as a worthy antagonist. He had repaired many of the disasters both in Flanders and Italy; he would have saved both Lille and Turin, had he not been hampered by a divided command, as well as by impracticable orders from the Court; and when, in 1711, he was summoned to take the command in Spain, his name acted like a charm—Spanish enthusiasm revived, soldiers flocked to his standard, and in a few months he recovered most of the lost ground in the Peninsula. It may be added to this that he was idolised by his own troops, and that his white plume was to be seen, like that of his grandfather, Henry of Navarre, in the thickest of the fighting.

Saint Simon tells us, with an ill-concealed air of triumph, how miserably Vendôme died, soon after his successes in Spain. Always a great epicure, he had retired, with a few attendants, to a little hamlet on the Spanish coast, and there he gorged himself with fish to such an extent that he actually died, like one of our English kings, "from a surfeit of lampreys." Every one abandoned him in his last moments, and his valets plundered him and decamped, taking with them even the mattress and bed-clothes, and leaving their unfortunate master, in spite of his piteous entreaties, to die alone on the bare boards. As he had deserved so well of Spain, Philip ordered his body to be taken to the Escurial—the palace and mausoleum of the Spanish kings—where it was walled up in one of the outer rooms. When Saint Simon visited the spot some years afterwards, he saw the last resting-place of his old enemy. "I gently asked the monk in charge," he says, "when the body was to be carried into the inner room; but they avoided satisfying my curiosity: indeed they showed some irritation, and did not scruple to let me understand that they did not think of moving it at all, and that, since they had done so much for him as to wall him up there, he might stay there altogether."

Louis had again made overtures of peace in 1710, and sent two ambassadors to a conference at Gertruydenburg—one of them being Polignac, the most skilful diplomatist of the day. As before, the French king was ready to make all reasonable concessions, but the Dutch demands were even more insolent than in the previous year. Louis must dethrone his grandson, they insisted, by force of arms, if persuasion failed. But this humiliation was more than Louis could brook. "Since one must make war," he said, "it shall be against my enemies, not against my children;" and his ambassadors left Holland, appealing "to God and to Europe against the sufferings and bloodshed that must follow from the obstinacy of Heinsius and the ambition of Marlborough."

Saint Simon moralises, after his own fashion, over the ignominy of these abortive negotiations, and on the deplorable calamities of the war that was desolating his country :—

"Led in this manner up to the very verge of the precipice, with a horrible deliberation that gave time to appreciate all its depth, that all-powerful hand which has placed a few grains of sand as a boundary to the most furious storms of the sea, arrested all at once the final destruction of this presumptuous and haughty monarch, after having made him taste, in long bitter draughts, all his feebleness, his misery, and his nothingness. It was some grains of sand of another kind—but still grains of sand in their insignificance—that brought to pass this master-work of Providence. A woman's quarrel about some trifles in the Court of Queen Anne and the intrigue that arose out of it, followed by a vague and unformed desire for the success of her own blood, detached England from the Grand Alliance."

The result of this quarrel between Queen Anne and her favourite was the disgrace of Marlborough and the return of the Tories to office, who at once reversed the aggressive policy of the Whigs and "held out a hand to France." In 1712, an unknown abbé suddenly presented himself before Torcy, charged with a verbal message from Bolingbroke. "Are you willing to make peace? I bring you the means of opening negotiations." It was, said Torcy, as if he had asked a dying man if he would like to recover his health. The preliminaries were soon settled, and in 1713 peace was actually concluded at Utrecht. This treaty, says Saint Simon, cost Spain half her kingdom. Philip retained the Spanish peninsula; but Naples, Milan, and Flanders were severed from his empire. France gave up all her border fortresses; and England gained Nova Scotia and Newfoundland. The following year a separate treaty was concluded with the emperor at Rastadt; and thus, at an infinite cost of men and money, and after nearly thirty years of incessant war, France found herself at last at peace with the nations round her.

CHAPTER X.

THE PROVINCES.

For the *grands seigneurs*, as we have seen, life in these days flowed on pleasantly and gracefully enough; but there is another side to this brilliant picture—"the reverse of the medal," as Saint Simon puts it. At the Court all was luxury and extravagance, and this while five armies were often in the field at once, and while Louis was squandering millions on his palace and *fêtes*. It cannot but be asked how this enormous drain on the wealth of the country was sustained, and how was the exchequer able to support the burden of war and peace? It was this question that had baffled every Minister of Finance since the time of Colbert,—for he alone seems to have realised the simplest axiom of political economy, ignored by those who succeeded him in office, that the only way of enriching the exchequer was by developing to their utmost the productive resources of the country. It was with this view that Colbert had encouraged manufactures, stimulated commerce, and done his utmost to give confidence to French merchants, and stability to the public credit of French bankers. And in this way he had solved the great problem of finance,—he had increased the revenue without increasing taxation.

But his successors had neither his genius nor his courage. They went back to all the pernicious expedients of Mazarin to raise money for the war. Every office and dignity in the state, from a marquisate to a captaincy, had its price, and was sold to the highest bidder. And when these were exhausted, new offices and new dignities were created and put up for auction. "Sire," said the Minister of the day to Louis, "when your Majesty creates a new office, God always creates a fool to buy it." Then they issued a large amount of paper money, and in consequence the currency was depreciated and prices were enhanced. Then they taxed every possible commodity—corn, and linen, and hemp, and silk; they placed custom-houses at every cross-road, and employed fifty thousand men incessantly in collecting these taxes from the wretched peasants. So heavy, indeed, were the taxes upon fluids of all kinds (*aides*), that while curiosities could be brought across the seas from Japan, and sold for only four times their value in Paris, a bottle of wine from the French provinces cost twenty times its value when it reached the Halles. It took three months and a half for the unfortunate wine-seller to pass his casks through the countless custom-houses that lined the highroads between Paris and Marseilles. In fact, both farmers and vine-growers found that it no longer repaid them to cultivate the soil. And thus the corn-fields of Languedoc, the vineyards of Anjou, the orchards of Normandy, were left untilled; and the figs and olives in Provence hung rotting on the trees. France, from one end to the other, looked like a country that had been wasted by war and pestilence. The peasants were seen shivering in rags and stripped of all that they possessed, huddled together upon straw or roaming through the fields, and flying from the presence of the tax-gatherer. After reading the terrible chapters in which Saint Simon has described their misery, it is easy to appreciate the irony of La Bruyère's picture of the same period.

"One sees certain savage animals, male and female, scattered over the country, of a livid hue, scorched and blackened by the sun, bound down to the soil which they constantly ransack and turn over with invincible obstinacy. These creatures have a sort of articulate voice, and when they raise themselves on their feet, they show a human face, and, in fact, they are—men. At night they hide themselves in their huts, where they live on black bread, water, and roots. They spare other men the trouble of sowing, and toiling, and reaping for a livelihood, and it is only reasonable that they should not want the bread which they have sown."

But these poor creatures could not even get this bread. Wheat was heavily taxed, and was not even allowed to pass from one province to another; the system of "monopolies" still further raised the price of corn, and while the bakers and Government agents were making fortunes, hundreds of the wretched peasants in the provinces were dying of hunger. This distress culminated in the winter of 1709, which was ushered in by a frost of such unusual severity that Saint Simon tells us not only did the Seine become a block of solid ice, but even the sea was frozen on the coasts, and carried loaded waggons on its surface. Half the olive-trees and vines in France were killed by the intense frost; the cattle perished for want of food; and the peasantry died in hundreds of cold, disease, and famine.

"At the same time the taxes—increased, multiplied, and exacted with the extremest severity—completed the desolation of France. Everything increased in price beyond belief, while nothing remained to buy with, even at the cheapest rate.

. . . .

"People did not cease wondering what could have become of all the money in the kingdom. No one could pay any longer, because no one got paid himself. The country people, owing to excessive taxation and bankrupt estates, had themselves become insolvent. Though all trade was taxed, it no longer yielded any profit; while public credit and confidence had completely disappeared. Thus the king had no resource except the terror and the custom of his boundless power, though even this, all illimitable as it was, itself failed for want of victims to seize and persecute. He no longer even paid his troops,—though, unless he did so, it is impossible to conceive what became of the countless millions that poured into his treasury.

"Such was the fearful state to which all France was reduced, when our ambassadors were sent into Holland [to negotiate a peace]. This picture is accurate, faithful, and not the least overdrawn. It was necessary to give it in its true colours, to explain the dire extremity to which we were reduced, the enormity of the concessions which the king allowed himself to make to obtain peace, and the visible miracle of Him who puts bounds upon the sea, and who calls things which are not to be as things which are,—by which He delivered France from the hands of Europe, ready and resolved to destroy her."

After reading these terrible chapters, in which Saint Simon describes the France of his day and which even now thrill the reader with indignation, it is easy to realise how all this misery and oppression, repeated and intensified through three successive reigns, produced at last the Revolution of 1789; and the only wonder is that the people should have suffered so patiently and endured so long. But, even in Saint Simon's time, we have warnings of the coming storm; we are told of risings among the peasantry which had to be suppressed by strong bodies of troops; of serious bread riots in Paris; of murmurs and execrations heard even under the windows of Versailles; of insulting placards affixed to the statues of the king; and of treasonable letters, some of which found their way to Louis himself, hinting that there were still Ravaillacs left in the world, and that a Brutus might yet be found to avenge the wrongs of a long-suffering country.

Some years before this, Vauban, perhaps the purest patriot as well as the most skilful engineer in France, had been profoundly touched by what he had seen of the state of the provinces as he went on official journeys from one fortress to another. The last twenty years of his life had been devoted to a personal inquiry into the trade, productions, and revenues of the country, and he had summed up his information in a volume which reviewed the existing system of taxation, exposed its abuses and enormities, and proposed to abolish the multifarious customs and duties, as well as the host of officials employed in collecting them. In their place Vauban would have had one grand tax — the "Royal Tithe"—to be levied partly upon land and partly upon trade; and thus some relief, he thought, would be given to the hard-working tillers of the soil,—a class "so despised, and yet so useful, which has suffered so deeply, and is suffering still."

But Vauban's scheme, like other sweeping measures of reform, clashed with the "vested interests" of the day. The whole army of collectors—from the controller-general down to the humblest clerk—saw at once that if it were carried into effect, the hope of their gains was gone, and they one and all joined in a strenuous opposition.

"This book," says Saint Simon, "had one great fault. Though it would, as a matter of fact, have given to the king more than he got by the modes of taxation in use up to that time; though it would have saved the people from ruin and distress, and would have enriched them by allowing them to enjoy, with a very slight exception, all that did not actually enter the king's treasury;—it would have ruined a host of capitalists, of agents, and *employés* of every sort; it would have forced *them* to seek a livelihood at their own expense, and no longer at that of the public, and would have sapped the foundations of those immense fortunes which we have seen spring up in so short a time. This was what checked the scheme of Vauban."

Chamillart, then Minister of Finance, gave way to the pressure put upon him by the privileged classes, and Louis himself was led to believe that Vauban's scheme was that of a meddlesome republican, whose views were at once mischievous and treasonable. Indeed, one sentence in the book was pointed out to him as intended to strike at the first principles of absolute monarchy. "It was unjust," Vauban had written, "that all the body should suffer to put one of its members at ease." Accordingly, when the Marshal presented his work to the king, he was received ungraciously, and was told in plain language that his views were dangerous and revolutionary; while the copies of his book were at once impounded by the police. This ingratitude from a monarch whom he had served only too well was a deathblow to the old man, then in his seventy-fourth year. He withdrew from Court in cruel disappointment, and a few weeks afterwards died at his country-house of a broken heart.

In one sense Vauban's scheme died with him; but it died only to be revived in a new form not many years afterwards. Desmarets had succeeded Chamillart as Minister of Finance, and had exhausted every apparent means of raising money, — doubling and trebling the capitation tax, and increasing the taxes on all commodities till they amounted to four times their value. At last, driven to his wits' end and (as Saint Simon puts it) "not knowing of what wood to make a crutch to lean upon," Desmarets proposed that the "Royal Tithe" should be levied upon all classes in addition to their other burdens, although when Vauban had proposed it by way of superseding every other tax, it had been rejected as something too monstrous to be put in force. A Commission was appointed to see if it was practicable, and they reported in favour of levying it. But, even then, Louis shrank back with something like horror from the idea of imposing this last burden on his subjects. However, to relieve his conscience he consulted Père Tellier, and that Jesuit, with the easy logic of his Order, assured him that the most learned doctors of the Sorbonne had unanimously agreed that the property of the people was really the property of the king, and that, if he confiscated it, he was, after all, only taking back what was properly his own.

Accordingly, this tax, "designed," says Saint Simon, "by a bureau of cannibals, was signed, sealed, and registered amid stifled sobs, and proclaimed amid most subdued but most piteous lamentations." No person in the state was exempt from it, and the odious inquisition into private incomes and property, necessary for its enforcement, made it still more detestable. Even the king's own family spoke of it with abhorrence, and contrasted such injustice with the paternal government of ancient times; they denounced it "with a holy anger that recalled the memory of Saint Louis, of Louis XII. the father of his people, and of Louis the Just." So heavy had the weight of taxation now become, that the province of Languedoc offered to give up its entire revenues to the Crown, on condition of being allowed to keep a tenth part clear of taxes. But this proposal was rejected as an insult.

The only practical result of this heavy imposition seems to have been that Louis was able to add five men to each company of his infantry; that the Carnival began earlier; and that, as if to drown care, the winter balls and *fêtes* at Marly were on a more splendid scale than ever. Yet all the while, adds our chronicler, "Paris did not remain the less sad, nor the provinces the less desolated."

CHAPTER XI.

MEUDON AND MONSEIGNEUR.

IT is scarcely possible to follow Saint Simon's Memoirs by summers and winters in the way Thucydides wrote his history, for the simple reason that our writer never troubled himself about chronological sequence, but tells his story as the fancy leads him, without any regard to method or arrangement—perhaps even thinking that such mechanical details belonged rather to "the men of the quill," whom he holds in such profound contempt, than to a *grand seigneur* like himself. It would be an endless task to keep step with him along his own track, as he wanders from subject to subject, and from one digression to another, breaking off from the stirring incidents of the war to describe some scandal at the Court, or to give the pedigree of some gentleman-in-waiting. All that can be done, if we attempt to follow him at all, is to select the more striking episodes and characters, and to disentangle the scattered threads of individual histories.

Leaving, therefore, for a while, the war and the provinces, and going back to Saint Simon's personal life at Court, it may be remembered that he often speaks with mingled fear and aversion of the "Meudon cabal." Meudon was Monseigneur's country-house, and "Monseigneur" was the name by which the Dauphin was always known. He resembled his father, says a writer, "as Vitellius might have resembled Julius Cæsar." He had the fine features of the Bourbons, but they were without expression and bloated by excess; he had the grand deportment, but it was disfigured by his corpulence; he had the majestic carriage, but halted in his walk. All the grand social qualities of Louis were vulgarised in his son. The king would play for large sums with a magnificent indifference as to whether he won or lost, and often paid the gambling debts of his courtiers. Monseigneur also played for high stakes, but always with a greedy anxiety to win what he could. The king had thrown a halo of romance over his amours, but Monseigneur's mistress was one Choin—" a great, fat, flat-nosed brunette"—who came by the back-stairs, and had the air and appearance of a servant-maid. "As to character," says Saint Simon, "Monseigneur had none."

"He was without vice or virtue, without talent or any sort of knowledge, and radically incapable of acquiring any. Extremely lazy, without imagination or originality, without refinement, without taste, without discernment; born to be the prey of a weariness which he imparted to others, and to be a stone set rolling haphazard by another's impulsion; obstinate and excessively mean in everything; easily prejudiced beyond all conception, and ready to believe everything he saw; given over to the most mischievous hands, and incapable of either extricating himself or perceiving his position; drowned in his fat and his mental blindness (*ténèbres*); so that, without wishing to do wrong, he would have made a pernicious king."

His ignorance, even for a Bourbon, was something surprising. He knew nothing whatever of any subject except cookery, could talk of nothing except his last boar-hunt, and read nothing except the list of births and deaths in the Gazette. He never took the slightest interest in politics or affairs of the day. Even when Lille was besieged, and, as we have seen, the Court was in a fever of anxiety for news from the seat of war, Monseigneur went out hunting as usual; and on coming back one afternoon, he recited a long list of strange names of places he had passed in the forest to the Princess de Conti. "Dear me! Monseigneur," said the lady, out of patience, "what a wonderful memory you have! It is a thousand pities you should load it with such trifles." He seems to have been incapable of deep feeling of any kind, and his heartlessness extended even to his own family. When the Court was plunged into consternation by the sudden death of "Monsieur," the king's brother, Monseigneur did not show the slightest emotion, but rode off to a wild-boar hunt; and even when his old friend and companion, the Prince de Conti, was on his deathbed, Monseigneur drove past his house, along one side of the Quai de Louvre, to the opera, while the priests were carrying the Sacrament to the dying man along the other side, without even stopping his carriage.

Except on State occasions, he rarely went to Versailles, if he could help it, for he was oppressed by the formality and decorum of the Court, and felt the piety of his son, the Duke of Burgundy, to be a kind of reflection on his own life; while, like the rest of the royal family, he never ventured to open his mouth in the king's presence. Indeed, Louis, whatever his private feelings may have been, never showed his son the least affection, and always, says Saint Simon, treated him "with the air of a king rather than a parent." His opinion was rarely asked, and his advice—if he offered it—was rarely acted upon, except perhaps in the solitary instance of the Spanish succession.

In spite of the vigorous health of Louis, and the fatal prediction made at his own birth — "son of a king, father of a king, never a king"—Monseigneur seems to have occasionally indulged in the idea of succeeding to the throne. Only a few months before his death, Saint Simon tells us that he was found turning over some prints of the coronation ceremony with two of his lady friends, who were eagerly pointing out the various personages. "See, there is the man who will put the spurs on for you, and that one will give you the royal mantle, and here are the peers who will place the crown on your head." The anecdote is worthless except as illustrating the innocent vanity of the man.

Monseigneur's happiest days were passed at his own chateau of Meudon, where he lived at his ease like an ordinary country gentleman, keeping open house, hunting daily in the forest, and filling up his time otherwise pleasantly enough; playing cards and talking, seated with the ladies of his little Court. There was never any want of society; in fact, Meudon, like Carlton House in the days of George III., became the headquarters of "the Opposition,"—a cave of Adullam, a house of refuge for all the gay and turbulent spirits who sought an escape from the constraints of Versailles. Gathered there might be found a brilliant and incongruous new society — "libertins," as Louis disdainfully called them — sceptics and freethinkers, wits like La Fare and Bussy Rabutin, beauties like Madame de Soubise and the two Lislebonnes, soldiers like Vendôme and Luxemburg, poets and abbés, statesmen and philosophers, all taking their part in the famous "parvulos" of Meudon.

The queen of this society was "Madame la Duchesse," to whose fascinations Saint Simon is obliged to do unwilling justice, much as he both feared and hated her; and associated with her was a name that carried with it a romantic interest, the Prince de Conti, a nephew of the great Condé.

"He was the constant delight of the world, of the Court, and of the army; the divinity of the people, the idol of the soldiers, the hero of the officers, the hope of all that was most distinguished in the army, the delight of the Parliament, the discriminating friend of the *savants*, and often the admiration of the Sorbonne, of lawyers, of astronomers, and of the profoundest mathematicians. He had talents of the finest kind—luminous, just, exact, vast, extensive—with an infinite knowledge of books,—one who forgot nothing and knew by heart all public and private histories and genealogies, their chimeras and their realities."

When he talked, we are told that young and old alike hung upon his words, that men forgot the dinner-hour, and left the royal circle in the drawing-room at Marly in their eagerness to listen. In his younger days Conti had burned to distinguish himself as a soldier, and had shown that he inherited something of Condé's spirit, when he charged at the head of the household troops and saved the day at Neerwinden. But Louis, according to Saint

Simon, was jealous of his brilliant talents,[1] and Conti found himself at the age of thirty the only prince of the blood-royal left without even the command of a regiment. This neglect preyed upon his mind, and, to drown his grief and disappointment, he plunged into the wildest dissipation, and when the coveted opportunity of distinction came at last, it was too late. His health had been undermined by his excesses, and he sank into a rapid decline. The crowds who filled the churches night and day offering prayers for his recovery, and the incessant stream of visitors that filled the ante-rooms of his house in Paris, showed how strong a hold his character had taken on public feeling. There must have been something singularly fascinating about this prince, when, in spite of his notorious profligacy, we find him spoken of with warm affection by such men as Fénelon and Bossuet, Chevreuse and Beauvilliers.

Saint Simon says of Conti—"This man, so charming, so amiable, so delightful, loved nothing; he had and desired friends as one has and desires furniture;" evidently forgetting that in another passage he has spoken of his strong affection for his sister-in-law, Madame la Duchesse,—an affection that was almost romantic in its constancy and hopelessness, and that ceased only with his death. Even when elected King of Poland, he was not sorry to give up the barren honour to the Elector of Saxony, and return to the charmed circle

[1] We give Conti's story as Saint Simon has given it, but he does not even allude to the scandal of 1686 (mentioned by both Madame de Maintenon and Madame de Sévigné), and which was probably the reason why the king always regarded this brilliant prince with such special disfavour. Conti was, if anything, a worse character than Vendôme.

at Meudon. "It was too much to expect," says Saint Simon, "that the brilliancy of a crown should prevail over the horrors of perpetual banishment."

Everything that was evil in Saint Simon's eye came from Meudon. The place was "beset with dangers and pitfalls" and "infested by demons." The brilliant society collected there were all so many personal enemies bent on his destruction. Madame la Duchesse regarded him with special animosity. He was at daggers-drawn both with Antin and Vendôme, two of the leading spirits in the cabal; and some busybody had told Monseigneur that Saint Simon had called him "a great imbecile, whom any one could lead by the nose," and, so far as Monseigneur's sluggish nature was capable of strong feeling, he showed strong and not unnatural indignation on the subject. As the king was now seventy-three, there seemed every probability that Monseigneur would succeed him before long; and to Saint Simon, who knew how completely the Dauphin was in the hands of the clique that made Meudon their headquarters, his prospects in the next reign were of the gloomiest description.

But an unexpected deliverance appeared. Saint Simon had gone down to keep Easter, as usual, at his country-house, when he heard that Monseigneur had been suddenly seized with the small-pox, and was lying between life and death at Meudon. Saint Simon tells us with what "an ebb and flow of emotion" he heard this news, and how "the man and the Christian struggled with the man of the world and the courtier." In a torment of uncertainty he left La Ferté and returned to Versailles; and there he heard that Monseigneur had so far recovered, that his friends the fishwomen of Paris had left their markets and come over in a body to congratulate their favourite prince. Saint Simon sought out the Duchess of Orleans (who, like himself, hated Meudon and all that belonged to it); and, as he puts it, "the drag was taken off their tongues in this rare conversation." With the utmost frankness they condoled with one another on the prospects of Monseigneur's recovery in spite of his age and corpulence; "and you may be certain," sadly added the Duchess, with a spark of the wit of Mortemart, "if his Highness once gets over the small-pox, there is not the faintest chance of his dying of apoplexy or indigestion."

But, even while Saint Simon and the Duchess of Orleans were thus charitably talking, a change had taken place for the worse at Meudon. Alarming symptoms suddenly showed themselves, and there was only just time to administer the last sacrament before Monseigneur lost consciousness, and an hour afterwards Fagon, the Court physician, announced that all was over.

The king had hurried from Versailles to Meudon at the first alarm of the Dauphin's danger, but the Princess of Conti met him in the doorway and prevented his entering the sick-room, for he had never had the small-pox himself. Then, overcome by the shock (for he had loved his son after a fashion), he sank fainting on a sofa in the ante-room, while Madame de Maintenon sat by his side giving him what comfort she could, and "tried hard to shed some tears herself." At last Louis was led to his coach, and drove off to Marly among a crowd of unfortunate valets and servants of Monseigneur's household, all crying out that they had lost their master, and must die of hunger.

It was nearly midnight when a courier arrived at Versailles with the news of Monseigneur's death; and Saint Simon has painted for us, as he only can paint, the details of the horribly grotesque scene that ensued when the long gallery was filled from end to end with crowds of half-dressed princes and courtiers roused from their beds; and he has described for us every posture, every attitude, and every gesture in the scattered groups —each countenance telling its own history, as he feasted his eyes on the rich study of human nature,—unmoved himself except by a lingering dread that the sick man might, after all, have recovered, and at the same time heartily ashamed of such an unworthy feeling. The valets, he says, could not contain their "bellowings," for they had lost a master "who seemed expressly made for them;" the greatest part of the courtiers— "that is, the fools—dragged out their sighs with their nails, and with dry and wandering eyes praised the departed prince." Some, again, remained buried in thought, and saying nothing; others evidently relieved, but hiding their happiness by an assumed air of sadness, —"but the veil over their face was transparent, and hid not a single expression." The Duke of Burgundy was strongly moved, and showed natural sorrow; the Duchess, graceful as usual, had a troubled air of compassion, "which every one took for grief, but she found extreme difficulty in keeping up appearances, and when her brother-in-law [the Duke of Berry] howled—she blew her nose;" the Duchess of Orleans, "whose majestic countenance told nothing;" her husband weeping violently in a back room, where Saint Simon found him, to his great amazement, and implored him to dry his eyes at once, " for every one who saw them red would consider it a most ill-timed comedy." Then there was the "Meudon cabal" plunged into bitter grief at the sudden downfall of their hopes and schemes,—the Duchess of Berry in particular "showing horror mingled with despair painted on her face—a kind of furious grief, based not on affection but on interest." Amidst it all,

" Madame,[1] arrayed in full dress, arrived on the scene howling, and, not knowing why or wherefore, flooded them all with her tears as she embraced them, and made the palace re-echo again with her cries, and presented the extraordinary spectacle of a princess who had put on her State dress at midnight to come and weep and lament among a crowd of women in their night-dresses, almost like masqueraders.

. . . .

" In the gallery there were several tent-bedsteads placed there for security, in which some of the Swiss guards and servants slept, and they had been put out as usual before the bad news came from Meudon. While some of the ladies were talking most earnestly, Madame de Castries, who touched one of the beds, felt it move, and was much terrified. A moment afterwards the ladies saw a great bare arm suddenly draw aside the curtain and disclose to them a stout honest Swiss guard between the sheets, half awake and utterly dumfoundered, and who took a long time to make out the company in which he found himself, though he stared intently at them all, one after the other ; and at last, not thinking it proper to get up in the midst of such a grand assemblage, he buried himself in his bed and drew the curtain again. Apparently the good fellow had gone to bed before anybody had heard the news, and had slept so profoundly ever since as to have only just awoke. The saddest sights are often liable to the most absurd contrasts. This sight made

---

[1] Monsieur's widow,—see p. 62.

all the ladies near the bed laugh, and caused some alarm to the Duchess of Orleans and her friends who had been talking with her, lest they should have been overheard; but, on reflection, they were reassured by the heavy slumber and stupidity of the fellow."

There was little sleep for any one else on that eventful night, and Saint Simon was himself astir again at seven in the morning; but, he says, "such restlessness is sweet, and such awakenings have a pleasant flavour of their own."

CHAPTER XII.

THE DUKE AND DUCHESS OF BURGUNDY.

THE nine months that followed Monseigneur's death was certainly the happiest period of Saint Simon's life. Not only was he free from a sense of impending evil from the "Meudon cabal," which, as we have seen, haunted him perpetually, but the young Duke of Burgundy, who now succeeded to his father's position as the Dauphin of France, became his intimate personal friend and supporter, and for the time being nothing could be brighter than his prospects. We are told that, when a boy, the new Dauphin had been passionate and wayward—furious with the weather when it rained, and breaking the clocks that struck the hour of his lessons; and his pride was such, says Saint Simon, that "he seemed to look down from the height of the heavens on men as mere atoms, to whom he bore no resemblance, and scarcely even acknowledged the princes, his brothers, as intermediate links between himself and the human race." But, happily for himself, he came under the good influence of Fénelon and Fleury at this crisis of his life, and "God, who is the master of hearts, and whose divine spirit breathes where He wills, made of this prince a work of His right hand, and he came forth from this abyss affable, gentle, humane, moderate, patient, modest, humble, and austere." He passed indeed from one extreme to the other, and his piety and reserve at times tried the patience of his best friends at Court. He refused to be present at a ball given at Marly on Twelfth Night, because it happened to be the Feast of the Epiphany as well; and once even Louis, when summoning him to a council of war, said ironically, "Come,—that is, unless you prefer going to Vespers." He lived at this time the life of a recluse, absorbed in study, and constantly reading the "Blue-books" of his day,—long treatises on finance, on commerce, and on the internal administration of France, prepared for him by practical statesmen like Chevreuse and Beauvilliers.

It was through the good offices of these veteran politicians that Saint Simon owed his introduction to the young prince. "For many years they never lost the opportunity," he says, "of inspiring him with feelings of friendship, esteem, and personal regard for me;" and then, with that warmth of affection which was as strong a feeling with him as his hatred, Saint Simon made an idol of the young prince, and credited him with being nothing less than perfection both in head and heart. As has been seen, he supported him warmly when attacked for his conduct during the campaign of 1708; he was never weary of enlarging on his talents and capacity to the small circle of devoted friends who had, like himself, great hopes of Fénelon's pupil; and, as Saint Simon was never happy unless he had a pen in his hand, it probably needed very little persuasion on the part of Beauvilliers to induce him to put on paper his views on what may be called the whole duty of a prince. It is an eloquent if a somewhat incoherent essay, and begins with a graceful compliment to Fénelon, whose hand "was so singularly formed by heaven to sow the good seed on a rich soil." What the Dauphin most required was that knowledge of the world that can never be gained from books or the companionship of "a troop of women." He must not carry his studies too far into life, much less waste his time on abstract science, on mechanics, or on frivolous experiments. He should leave such vanities to priests and recluses, and apply himself instead to the one master-science—that of government —to which all other sciences are but as stepping-stones. He should talk less to his confessor, and more to the statesmen and politicians of his day; he should make friends with men of different classes, and learn from each and all lessons of real life that would be of more value to a future king than all the folios of the Jesuits or all the learning of the Sorbonne; and he should gather this practical knowledge from the best men of their class, "as bees gather the sweetest honey from different flowers." And thus he would become himself, as a true prince should be, "an epitome of the State."

The Dauphin's character seems to have received a fresh impulse after Monseigneur's death. He left his study and his books, and began to mingle freely in society, talking sensibly and agreeably, and charming all alike by his polite and graceful manner. "He became a second Prince de Conti; people opened their eyes and ears, and asked one another if this was the same man they had known before, and if it was a dream or a reality."

The king showed him every mark of confidence; the Ministers had orders to take their portfolios to him, and acquaint him with all public business; and we are told that in their turn they were astonished, though not altogether delighted, at the variety and depth of his information. As to Saint Simon, this change was like the realisation of some delightful dream. Here was a prince such as his fancy had pictured, impressed like himself with a sense of the dignity of the ducal order, of the usurpations of the "bourgeoisie" and the "bastards," and of the necessity of reconstructing society on the old lines of feudalism. The prince and the duke had long interviews, in which they discussed and arranged the policy of the future; but these interviews were kept a profound secret from all the world. But one afternoon

"The sitting was a long one, and after it ended we sorted our papers. He gave me some of his to put in my pocket, and he took some of mine. He shut them up in his desk, and instead of putting the rest in his bureau he left them outside, and began to talk with his back to the fireplace—his papers in one hand and his bag in the other. I was standing up near the bureau looking for certain papers, and holding some others in my hand, when all at once the door opened opposite me and the Dauphiness entered.

"The first *coup d'œil* of all three of us—for, thank heaven! she was alone—the astonishment painted on our three faces, have never left my memory. This fixed stare, this statue-like immobility, this silence and embarrassment in all three of us, lasted longer than a slow *Pater*. The princess broke it first. She said to the prince in a very discomposed voice, that she did not think he was in such good company— smiling at him and then at me. I had time to smile also, and then lower my eyes before the Dauphin answered. 'Since you find me so, madame,' said he, smiling at the same time, 'be off with you.' She stood an instant looking at him and smiling still more, and he at her, and then she turned a pirouette, went out, and closed the door, for she had not passed beyond the threshold.

"Never did I see a woman so astonished; never (and I must use a slang expression) did I see a man so dumfoundered (*penaud*) as the prince even after she had gone; never was a man—for I must confess it—in such a terrible fright as I was at first, though I felt reassured as soon as I saw that she was not followed. As soon as she had shut the door—'Well, sir,' said I to the Dauphin, 'if you had only chosen to draw the bolt!' 'You are right,' said he, 'and I was wrong; but there is no harm done. Luckily she was by herself, and I will answer for her secrecy.' 'I am not at all troubled,' said I—although I was mightily afraid all the time—'but it is a miracle that she came by herself. If her suite had been with her, you would perhaps have got off with a scolding, but I should have been irrecoverably ruined.'"

However, the Dauphiness kept the secret, and in future these two conspirators were more cautious in their interviews, though they still met frequently, and built their castles in the air with all the ardour of young reformers. The key-note of their system was a sentence which the Dauphin had ventured to utter even in the drawing-room at Marly—that "kings are made for the people, and not the people for the king." Society was to be reorganised on a more just and liberal basis in the next reign. The long ascendancy of the "*vil bourgeois*" was to come to an end; there were to be no more plebeian Ministers like Colbert and Torcy, no more officers and governors drawn from "the Third Estate;" the powers of the old aristocracy were to be revived; a council of sixty was to take the place of the Cabinet of six; the abuses of centuries were to be swept away; all citizens were to be equal before the law, and share equally in the burdens of taxation; there was to be a new France and a new people, not worn out with toil and misery, but free, contented, and industrious; and above them, tier upon tier, were to rise the ranks of the peerage, culminating in the DUKES, second to royalty alone, and "the most precious jewels of the crown." And, as in Plato's Republic nothing was needed for its fulfilment but a prince who should be a philosopher as well, so in Saint Simon's Utopia all was to be realised when the Dauphin became a king. The Duke of Burgundy was to be "the second Ezra, who should restore the temple, and lead back the people of God after their long captivity."

The young Duchess of Burgundy was far more popular than her husband. She had brought with her to the jaded Court at Versailles all the freshness and spirit of a young girl of seventeen, and lighted up every corner of the gloomy palace like sunshine on a winter's day. Louis himself almost idolised her, and showed her far more affection than he had ever shown to his own children. A letter of his addressed to Madame de Maintenon is still preserved, in which he graphically describes how greatly her first appearance had delighted him; and he dwells upon her charms much as a veteran trainer would describe the points of some promising young colt. But her personal beauty was not so striking as her charming figure, her sweet expression, and her graceful carriage. "Her walk," says Saint Simon, "was that of a goddess over clouds. The Graces sprang up of themselves at every step she took. They adorned all her manners and her simplest words." [1]

Madame de Maintenon undertook her education, for she was hardly twelve years old when she arrived at Versailles, and she was constantly with her and Louis—indeed, the old king was never happy when the young girl was out of his sight. She would amuse him with her lively stories; would talk "slang" (*baragouinage*) in her Italian way; caress him, pinch him, turn over his papers, read his letters, mimic the Ministers almost to their faces, and interrupt the gravest conversation with some gay remark. One day Louis was talking to Madame de Maintenon over the chances of peace at the accession of Queen Anne. "My aunt," said the Dauphiness, "you must allow that the queens govern better than the kings in England; and do you know why, my aunt?" Then, skipping about the room all the while, she went on—"Because under kings it is the women who govern, and the men under the queens." The best of it was, continues Saint Simon, that both the king and Madame de Maintenon laughed heartily, and said she was right.

Nothing can be tenderer or more graceful than Saint Simon's picture of the young duchess who had won all their hearts; and he passes lightly over her indiscretions, though one flirtation (innocent enough on her side) had a strangely tragical ending. The disappointed lover—an Abbé Maulevrier—grew so frantically jealous of his

---

[1] Saint Simon, consciously or unconsciously, is translating Propertius. Those who wish to see a more modern translation of these famous lines should consult Sir A. Helps's 'Realmah' (i. 266).

supposed rival, a young captain in the Guards, that, after a hundred follies, he went raving mad, threw himself from a window in his delirium, and was miserably dashed to pieces. The young princess shed some bitter tears at the time, and did not recover her usually gay spirits for weeks afterwards. Yet neither her husband nor the king ever guessed the true reason of Maulevrier's death, and the secret, if there was one, was faithfully kept by those who knew it. Even in that Court of scandal and intrigue she had not made an enemy. "Ah, my dear Duke!" wrote Madame de Maintenon to De Noailles after her death, "who, indeed, that ever knew her, could help loving her?"

"One evening, at Fontainebleau, when the ladies and princesses were in the same room as herself and the king after supper, she had been talking nonsense in all kinds of languages, and said a hundred childish things to amuse the king, who delighted in them, when she noticed the two princesses of Condé and Conti looking at her, making signs to one another, and shrugging their shoulders with an air of contempt and disdain. The king rose and passed into a back room to feed his dogs, and the Dauphiness then took Madame de Saint Simon by one hand, and Madame de Levy by the other, and pointed to the two princesses, who were only a few paces from them. 'Did you see? did you see?' said she; 'I know just as well as they do that there is no common-sense in what I have just done and said, and that it is all wretched stuff: still, one must make a noise, and this sort of thing amuses him' (the king). Then, all at once, leaning on their arms, she began to dance and sing. 'Ha, ha! I laugh at it all! Ha, ha! I make fun of them, and I shall be their queen, and I have nothing to do with them either now or ever after, and they will have to reckon with me, and I shall be their queen,' still jumping and skipping about, and playing the fool with all her might. Her two ladies begged her, in a low voice, to keep quiet, or the princesses would hear her, and all the people in the room would see her doing this. They even went so far as to say she was out of her mind, for she heard nothing but good advice from them; but she only began to dance more vigorously, and sing in a louder tone, ' Ha, ha ! I make fun of them ! I don't care for them, and I shall be their queen.' And she only ceased when the king re-entered the room.

"Alas ! she believed it all—this charming princess—and who would not have believed it with her ? It pleased God for our misfortunes to rule it otherwise, not long after this scene, She was so far from thinking of it herself, that on Candlemas-day, being alone with Madame de Saint Simon, she began to talk of the number of persons at Court whom she had known and who had died, and then of what she would do herself when she grew old, and of the life she would lead, and how there was scarcely any one left about her of the time of her own youth.

. . . .

"With her were eclipsed all joy, pleasure, and even amusement and every kind of grace. Darkness covered the surface of the Court ; she had animated it all,—had filled all places at once ; her presence had occupied and penetrated every corner of it. If the Court existed after her, it was only to languish. Never was a princess so regretted, and never was there one more worthy of regret. So the regret for her has never passed away, and involuntary and secret bitterness of heart has abided with us, together with a frightful void that nothing can fill up."

Her death took place early in the year 1712. According to Saint Simon, she had been in perfect health up to that time, but had rashly taken some Spanish snuff given her by the Duke of Noailles, and the same evening she was attacked by an acute pain in the temples, followed by a violent fever. For several days her sufferings were intense, and she gradually lost strength, as this mysterious disease fastened upon her system. The doctors tried the severe remedies then in fashion—opium, bleeding, and emetics—but without success. The fever increased, and, "like a devouring fire," says Saint Simon, "preyed upon her night and day." She was induced to make her last confession, though she would not make it to her own confessor; the prayers for the dying were said over her; the Sacrament was administered; and soon afterwards she sank into a stupor from which she never rallied.

It was known that the Dauphin was sickening of the same terrible fever, but, as long as he could stand, he could not be induced to leave his wife's bedside. For the first few days of her illness he bore up against his sufferings, but at last his strength gave way, and he was carried to his rooms at Marly. Saint Simon saw him there for the last time, and was terrified at his wild and haggard looks, and at the livid marks on his face.

"His attendants proposed to him, once or twice, to go to the king's room, but he neither moved nor answered. I drew near and made him signs to go, and then proposed it to him in a low voice. Seeing that he still stayed and kept silence, I ventured to take him by the arm, to represent to him that, sooner or later, he must see the king,—that his Majesty was expecting him, and sorely desired to see and embrace him; and pressing him thus, I took the liberty to gently push him on. He threw on me a look that pierced me to the heart, and went. I followed him a few paces, and tore myself away from the spot to gather breath. I never saw him again from that moment. May it please God in His mercy that I may see him eternally, where his goodness has doubtless placed him!"

The king embraced his grandson "tenderly, long, and many times, their words being almost choked by tears and sobs;" and, immediately after the interview, the prince was carried to his bed, and he never left it again. The same deadly fever that had carried off his wife had now attacked the husband. He lingered, as she had done, some four days in great agony, until death released him from his sufferings.

Scarcely a month afterwards both his young children sickened of the measles; the elder died, and the younger brother's life was only saved by most careful nursing. The little child, who thus escaped, lived to become afterwards Louis XV.

Thus, three Dauphins had died within a year, and the strangely sudden manner of their deaths revived those horrible suspicions that had hung about the Duke of Orleans all his life. He was now credited with being a wholesale murderer, in addition to his other sins. His notorious impiety, his scandalous life, and the hours passed by him in his laboratory, all served to strengthen the popular belief that he had deliberately poisoned the Dauphin, the Dauphiness, and their young child, to clear his own way to the throne of France. Medical evidence, also, seemed to point in the same direction; for the seven doctors who had examined the bodies declared that some subtle and virulent poison must have been the cause of death, with the exception of Maréchal, who was firm in his opinion that it was a by no means unusual case of typhoid fever.

After being embalmed and lying in state, the remains of the Dauphin and Dauphiness were carried to their last resting-place in the Abbey of St Denis. As the *cortège* passed by torchlight along the Rue St Honoré into the broad square of the Palais Royal, the crowds who lined the streets gave way to tears and sobs of grief; but when the face of Orleans was seen through the window of his coach, there was a furious uproar, for his presence in the procession was felt by all to be a sacrilege to the dead. Curses and execrations were heard on all sides; sticks were shaken and stones were thrown; and, had not the Swiss Guards thrust back the mob with their halberds, Saint Simon believes that the Duke would then and there have been torn to pieces.

But, with all his vices, Philip of Orleans was not a murderer. He was both soft-hearted and affectionate, and was, in his own way, attached to his young cousin, though their characters were so utterly unlike. After the Dauphin's death he had been found by some of the attendants stretched upon the ground, and sobbing as if his heart would break. But at Court no one believed in his innocence. Rumours of the strangest kind were spread to his discredit. It was said that a monk who had actually administered the poison had been arrested by the prefect of police; that his own wife was to be the next victim, and that the Duke then intended to marry the widow of the King of Spain. He indignantly demanded a public trial, and to be confronted with his accusers, and defied the judgment of his peers and the Bastille itself, insisting that, in justice to the blood of Henry IV., France must be convinced of his innocence. Louis only shrugged his shoulders. "I can tell you," he coldly answered, " that the only accusers you have with me are your own immorality and frightful laxity of principle." At Court he was shunned like a pariah,—no one would come near him or speak to him; and at last his solitude grew so insupportable that he left Versailles, and took up his quarters again in the Palais Royal, where, says Saint Simon, it seemed to be a wager between himself and his daughter (the Duchess of Berry) which of them could scandalise most both religion and morality.

Saint Simon was himself plunged in the most bitter grief by the sudden loss of the young prince. At first he was inconsolable. He shut himself up in his rooms, and would see no one: indeed, had it not been for his wife, he would have left the Court altogether, and retired to his country-seat. The light of heaven, he says, seemed to have faded from the earth; the hand of death had robbed him of the most cherished and precious object of his life. His pathetic burst of sorrow recalls another occasion, when the heir of a great empire was suddenly cut off in the fulness of his youth and promise; and Saint Simon's lament over the Duke of Burgundy echoes the spirit and almost the words of Virgil's lament over the young Marcellus. "You have just come back," he said to Beauvilliers after the funeral, "from burying the fortunes of France. She has fallen under this last chastisement. God showed her a prince whom she did not deserve; the earth was not worthy of him; he was already ripe for eternal blessedness."

> "Ostendunt terris hunc tantum fata, neque ultra
> Esse sinunt."[1]

---

[1] Fénelon wrote to Beauvilliers in much the same tone. "God," he says, "has taken from us all our hopes for Church and State. He had prepared this young prince for the noblest ends, and had shown him to the world, only to take him almost immediately to Himself."

CHAPTER XIII.

THE LAST DAYS OF LOUIS XIV.

EVEN at this lapse of time there is something sad in reading Saint Simon's account of the last few years of the great king's reign. We feel—as Louis felt himself—that he has lived too long; that it would have been better for his fame to have died at the height of his glory and prosperity, than to have seen his country impoverished and exhausted by foreign war; to have seen the great names that had made his reign so famous, one after the other disappear from history; and to have seen his family through three generations go down to the grave before him. Death had been busy on all sides of him in these latter years. He had lost his wife, his only brother, his son, his favourite grandson, and above all his grandson's wife, the Duchess of Burgundy, whose death had created a void at Versailles which nothing could fill up. The great palace was like a desert without her, and with her the life and sunshine of the Court seemed to have passed away for ever. It was in vain that Madame de Maintenon tried every means of cheering Louis at this melancholy time. Musical evenings at the Trianon, scenes from Molière's plays, conversations with his valets, the last new scandal, the last ill-natured jest of Lauzun, the last long story told by Villeroy,— all the trifles that had occupied and interested him had lost their charm. "What a punishment," wrote his weary favourite, "to have to amuse a man who is no longer amusable!"

In some ways the king, though he had passed his seventieth year, still kept the vigour and energy of former days. He would ride and drive for hours in the snow and rain; he would make his periodical journeys from Versailles to Marly, and from Marly to Fontainebleau; and he would still give audiences to ambassadors, work whole mornings with his Ministers, and preside at councils of State. But when the work of the day was over, the long evenings passed in Madame de Maintenon's room became more and more insupportable both to him and to her. She had grown deaf and almost blind—"a living skeleton," she calls herself—and the two would sit for hours silent, forlorn, and brooding over the memories of the past, their solitude only broken by the arrival of a Minister with his tale of some fresh distress in the provinces; by Fagon, the doctor, now bent double with age, but with all his former bitterness of tongue; or by Père Tellier, the Jesuit, with his evil face and hateful insinuations.

There seemed to be a curse upon the house of Bourbon, for the Duke of Berry—the best and gentlest of the family—died suddenly at the age of twenty-eight. His horse had stumbled while he was out hunting, and thrown him so violently against the pommel of the saddle, that he bled to death from some internal injury. The heir was now the king's great-grandson, a feeble and sickly child four years of age.

To add to the old king's troubles, a new clique was formed to divert the Regency and possible chance of succession to the throne from the Duke of Orleans to the Duke of Maine, the favourite son of Louis by Madame de Montespan. From his boyhood Maine had been petted and caressed by Madame de Maintenon; and when he grew up, honours and wealth without end had been showered upon "this viper on the hearth," as Saint Simon calls him. One Act of Parliament had removed the bar-sinister from his shield, a second had given him precedence of all the dukes in the peerage, and a third had placed him within the charmed circle of princes of the blood-royal, and made him capable of succeeding to the throne as if he had been one of the true "sons of France." Some years before his death, Louis had made a personal appeal to his son and grandson to protect Maine and his children, to whom he had just extended all the privileges enjoyed by their father; and he made the elder of them, aged ten, colonel of the Swiss Guards, and the younger, aged six, Master of the Artillery.

"When this had been decided by the king — that is to say, between him and Madame-de Maintenon — the point was to declare it; and this declaration produced the strangest and most singular scene of any that occurred in all that long reign to any one who knew the king, and his intoxication with the sense of absolute sovereignty. When he entered his private room at Versailles on Saturday night, March 15th, after supper, and had given his customary orders, he advanced gravely into the anteroom, placed himself in front of his chair without sitting down, slowly passed his eyes over the whole company, and said to them, without addressing any one in particular, that he gave the children of the Duke of Maine the same rank and honours as their father; and, without a moment's interval, walked to the end of the cabinet, and called to him Monseigneur and the Duke of Burgundy. Then, for the first time in his life, this monarch so haughty, this father so severe, and such a master in his house, humbled himself before his son and grandson. He told them that, in view of their both successively reigning after him, he prayed them to acquiesce in the rank which he had bestowed on the children of the Duke of Maine,—to concede so much in consideration of the affection which he flattered himself they felt for him, and he for these children and for their father. He added that, at his great age, and considering that his death could not be far distant, he earnestly recommended them to their care in the most pressing manner he could, and he trusted that after his own death they would protect them out of regard for his memory."

Both princes remained dumb with astonishment, and the king again implored them to promise that it should be so.

"The two princes looked at one another, scarcely knowing whether what was passing was a dream or a reality, without answering a word the whole time, until, as they were still more earnestly entreated by the king, they stammered out something or other, without giving a distinct promise. The Duke of Maine, embarrassed by their embarrassment, and much mortified that no distinct answer had passed their lips, threw himself down so as to embrace their knees. It was then that the king, with his eyes swimming in tears, implored them to allow the Duke to embrace them in his presence, and to reassure him by that mark of friendship. He still continued to press them to give their word, while the two princes, more and more astonished by this extraordinary scene, still kept muttering what they could, but without promising anything definitely."

This remarkable scene had taken place while there was still every reasonable prospect of Louis being succeeded by his son or grandson. But the sudden death of two Dauphins had considerably narrowed the circle of direct heirs; and in the event of the little child called the Duke of Anjou also dying, the crown of France would have gone to the Duke of Orleans. But this last enactment of 1710 had made it possible for the Duke of Maine to step in to the succession; and it was the chance of this that filled up the measure of Saint Simon's indignation. He declared that for a king thus to degrade the sacred dignity of his crown by making the succession "despotically arbitrary," and to give to a bastard the privileges of a crown-prince, was "a crime and a sacrilege blacker, vaster, and more terrible than high treason itself." And after enumerating no less than fifty-seven successive stages by which Louis had extended the privileges of his natural children—"after reading this," Saint Simon concludes, "one will be less struck by the imagination of those poets who made the giants pile mountain upon mountain to scale the heavens."

This may be so; but what strikes an impartial observer most, after reading this violent invective, is, that it was Saint Simon himself who was piling Ossa on Pelion—or rather, making mountains of molehills—in such a display of exaggerated indignation; as, after all, Louis was only exercising the right of adoption, which has been a recognised prerogative of monarchy since the days of the Roman emperors,—it might almost be said, since the time of the patriarchs. Certainly, in the case of the Bourbons, as in the case of the Stuarts, the king's natural children seem to have inherited more of the ancestral spirit than those born in the purple. Maine and his brother Toulouse were as superior in talent to Burgundy and Berry, as Monmouth and Berwick were to the unfortunate James II. or the still more unfortunate "Pretender."

But Saint Simon's prejudices will not allow to Maine the possession of a single virtue. He was as false and unscrupulous, we are told, as Madame de Maintenon herself, and imposed upon Louis by an affected piety and simplicity,—"so little did the king realise what a rattlesnake he was cherishing in the bosom of his family." But even all that had been already done for Maine did not satisfy him or his friends, and some further official sanction was needed to secure his future sovereignty. Accordingly, Père Tellier and Madame de Maintenon never rested, night and day, until by a sort of moral torture they had forced Louis to ratify with his own signature what Saint Simon calls "an enormous crime." They played upon his fears of poison, which had haunted him ever since the Duchess of Burgundy's death, and they made his life miserable to him, until at last he gave way. One morning the Procureur-General and the President of Parliament were summoned to Versailles, and the king solemnly handed them a document "sealed with seven seals." It was (he said with a weary sigh) his will, which he had been induced to sign as the price of his repose; it would probably be set aside after his death, like the wills of his predecessors, but such as it was, they must take it and guard it safely: and now he trusted he should be allowed to die in peace.

The astonished Ministers took the will, and solemnly deposited it, with all the security that iron bolts and doors could give, in a tower of the Palace of Justice at Paris. But though it had been so carefully sealed, its contents were generally known. Orleans was to be nominally Regent; but all real authority was to be vested in a council composed of the personal friends and adherents of Maine, who was himself to be the tutor and governor of the young king.

But in spite of his prospects of future grandeur, Maine was by no means easy in his mind. Between the princes and the peers, he felt that he might be crushed at any moment. "The sword of Dionysius hung by a hair above his head," says Saint Simon, grandiloquently; and his sense of insecurity made him seek allies on all sides. He first made overtures to the councillors in the Parliament, and then to the dukes, promising great things apparently to both, but, if we may believe Saint Simon, only with the intention of embroiling the two parties in a personal quarrel. He had bribed the First President, he had cajoled the Parliament, he had deceived the peers with the false pretence of taking their side; but, after all, his perfidy had been found out. "He devoted himself to the powers of darkness, and the very powers of darkness would not receive him." Saint Simon had an interview with him, and spoke out his mind (if we may take his own account) with his customary freedom.

"All at once, looking at him straight between the eyes—'It is you, sir, who have engaged us [the dukes] in this affair, in spite of ourselves; it is you who have answered for the king, for the First President, and for the Parliament; and lastly, it is you, sir, who have broken your word, and who have made us the plaything of the Parliament, and the laughing-stock of the world.'

"The Duke of Maine, usually so fresh-coloured and so easy in manner, became silent, and pale as a corpse. He would have stammered out excuses, and expressed his regard for the dukes, and for me in particular. I listened to him without taking my eyes off his for a single moment; and then, at last, fixing my eyes more and more intently on him, I interrupted him, and said in a high and haughty tone, but all the time tranquilly and without anger: 'Sir, you are all-powerful,—you show it both to us and to all France; enjoy your power, and all that you have obtained: but' (raising my head and my voice, and looking into the very depths of his heart) 'sometimes occasions come when one repents too late of having abused one's power, and of having mocked and deceived in cold blood all the principal nobles of the realm, and this they will never forget.'

"Thereupon I brusquely rose, and turned to go without giving him a moment for reply. The Duke of Maine, with an air of utter astonishment, and perhaps of vexation as well, followed me, still stammering out excuses and compliments. I continued to walk on, without turning my head, as far as the door. There I turned round, and said to him with an air of indignation: 'Oh sir! to escort me to the door after what has passed is to add mockery to insult.' At the same moment I passed through the doorway, and walked off without once looking behind me."

The person whose interests were most affected by this "exaltation of the bastard" was undoubtedly the Duke of Orleans; but Orleans, with his easy and careless temper, was the last man to be personally moved by it. He was to a certain extent conscious of the dangers surrounding him; but it was difficult to tell whom he could trust, or what steps he could take to strengthen his position. Even his own wife was supposed to favour her brother's (Maine's) claims. "We are lost in a wood," he said to Saint Simon, "and cannot take too much care of ourselves." And then he tried to forget his anxieties in the dissipations of Saint Cloud and the Palais Royal.

But, fortunately for him, his friends had more energy of character; and forward among them was his tutor, the Abbé Dubois, and, it need hardly be said, Saint Simon. They took decisive steps to rally their party round them. They secured on their side the great Marshals of France, the peers, the princes of the blood, the Jansenists, and many of the clergy, the Parliament, whose members had been slighted by Louis and duped by Maine, and lastly, the household troops—a picked body of ten thousand men—were to be kept in readiness, in case of a *coup d'état*, that, like the Prætorian Guards of old, they might decide the fate of the empire with their swords.

Frequent conferences of Orleans's friends were held, and their future policy discussed at length. As usual, Saint Simon was ready with a model constitution, much like the one he had before proposed to the young Duke of Burgundy. The Secretaries of State—"that tyranny of five kings"—were to be abolished, and a council of sixty was to take their place; the nobility were to be reinstated in their ancient privileges; the whole army of Government officials were to be sent about their business; and as the only means of extricating the country from the enormous debts contracted during the late war, a national bankruptcy was to be declared at once, since, in a choice of evils, it was better that the loss should fall on the capitalists—"those voracious animals that had preyed upon the vitals of their country."

Their opponents, Saint Simon thought, should be treated with toleration, except that " the bastards" should be deprived of their ill-gotten honours. As to the Jesuits, it would be sufficient if Père Tellier was civilly dismissed to the college of La Flêche; and if Lallemand and Doucin—" the firebrands of the plot and most dangerous scoundrels"—were shut up in Vincennes without pens, ink, or paper. As to Madame de Maintenon, "there was nothing more to be feared from that fairy of nearly eighty; her powerful and fatal wand had been broken, and she had once more become the widow Scarron." Beyond allowing her personal liberty and a competence, all credit and consideration should be taken from her. She had deserved far worse treatment than this, both from the State and the Duke of Orleans.

At last the event which both parties had been so anxiously expecting came to pass. In the summer of 1715 the king's health showed signs of rapid decline. His appetite, usually so good, began to fail him; he lost flesh; and it seemed that the diet of strong soups and spiced meats prescribed by his physician, followed by a quantity of fruits and sweetmeats, had impaired his digestive powers. His own courtiers noticed his changed appearance, and wagers were openly laid at the Hague and at St James's that he would not live another three weeks. Still Fagon, his physician, persisted that there was no real danger.

But on the 10th of August, as he was walking in the gardens of Versailles, he suddenly staggered, and had to be carried into the palace, and his serious illness could no longer be concealed. Still he held his council and gave audience as usual, although it was noticed when he received the Persian ambassador, that he tottered under the weight of his robes. He even persisted in being carried to hear Mass, and was present at a concert in Madame de Maintenon's room; and, as he was being wheeled along one of the corridors, he met Madame de Saint Simon, who had been away from Court for a fortnight, and with his usual courtesy stopped his chair and spoke to her: but she declared afterwards that she should hardly have recognised the king, so terribly had his appearance changed in the last ten days.

On the 24th he dined in public for the last time, and was evidently growing weaker. But still he clung to life. On the Sunday the drums and hautboys were ordered to play as usual under his windows—for it was the Feast of Saint Louis—and his stringed band performed in the ante-chamber during dinner. But the same evening he was seized with a kind of fit, and his mind began to wander; and so critical did his state appear to his doctors that Père Tellier and the Cardinal de Rohan were hastily summoned to his room, and he made his last confession and received the last Sacrament. Immediately afterwards he added a codicil to his will.

All day the galleries and ante-chambers were filled with a crowd of anxious courtiers, talking in low whispers, and trying to learn something from the valets and doctors who passed incessantly backwards and forwards from the room where the king was lying. His own dignity and presence of mind never left him. "Why do you weep?" he said to some of the princesses; "did you believe me to be immortal? Must I not pay to God the tribute of my life which is His due?" He had a last interview with the Duke of Orleans, and then summoned the gentlemen of his household to bid them farewell. With his usual grace of manner he thanked them all for their attachment and faithful services, and hoped they would be equally dutiful to the young king; and seeing some of them shedding tears, he added: "I see that I have affected you, and I am also affected myself. It is time for us to part. Adieu, gentlemen! I trust you will think of me sometimes."

"Then he ordered the little Dauphin to be brought to his bedside: 'My child, you are going to be a great king. Do not imitate me in the taste I have had for building and for war; strive, on the contrary, to be at peace with all your neighbours. Render to God what is His due; remember the obligations you are under to Him, and cause your subjects to honour Him. Follow good counsels, and try to be a comfort to your people, which I unfortunately have never been myself. Remember all that you owe to Madame de Ventadour'" (the governess).

He took the boy in his arms and embraced him tenderly. "My dear child, I give you my blessing with all my heart!"—more than once shedding tears himself—and the poor little prince (he was scarcely five years old) was then carried away by his governess, weeping bitterly.

Then Louis turned to Madame de Maintenon, and, pressing her hand, said, "What consoles me most of all is the hope that we may soon meet again!" "But this tender compliment," says Saint Simon, "displeased this ancient fairy, who, not content with being queen, apparently wished to be immortal as well." At the time, indeed, she made no reply, but afterwards remarked to her servant, Nanon—" A fine rendezvous he has given me ! This man has never loved any one but himself ! " And then she ordered her carriage and drove off to Saint Cyr.

The approaching death of the king had emptied the corridors and galleries of Versailles, and all the courtiers had thronged the rooms of the Duke of Orleans. But suddenly a rumour came that the king had rallied, and back they all rushed at once to the royal apartments. Orleans was amused at this trait of human nature. " My dear duke," he said to Saint Simon, who came to see him in his solitude, "you are the first person I have seen to-day ; " and he added, laughingly, " If the king eats again, we shall see nobody but ourselves."

The doctors had brought Louis an elixir, said to be of marvellous efficacy, which a countryman had persuaded them to give him. " Sire, it will restore you to life." " I neither desire nor hope to live," replied the king, and he drank the potion with indifference—"for life or for death," he said, " as it shall please God." The drug, whatever its secret virtues were, seemed to arrest for a time the progress of the disease ; but the relief was only temporary, and the gangrene, which had already shown itself in his limbs, spread upwards, and gradually paralysed his system. He was now conscious only at intervals, and it was seen that death must be very near. " You can go," said the confessor to Madame de Maintenon, who had been hastily summoned from Saint Cyr

—"you are no longer necessary to him;" and she accordingly left Versailles for the last time.[1]

The king's calmness, in the intervals when he was conscious, seemed extraordinary even to his physicians. Was it, as they suggested, that his malady had deadened all mental as well as bodily sensation; or was it, as others supposed, that he had been affiliated to the Order of the Jesuits, and that the "plenary benediction" he received from them had soothed and tranquillised his spirit?

The prayers for the dying were now said over him, and he joined in the responses with a voice still so strong and clear that it was heard above the voices of the priests around him. Then, as his sufferings grew more terrible, he was heard repeating incessantly to himself: "*Nunc et in horâ mortis*—Have pity on me, O my God! come to my aid! hasten to succour me!" These were his last audible words. All that night he still lingered on in his last agony, and it was not till past eight o'clock on the following morning that death at length released him. The Jesuit, who had never left his bedside, placed a crucifix on his breast; an officer in attendance stopped the palace clock at the fatal moment; a herald threw open the windows of the chamber, stepped out upon the balcony, and, in accordance with immemorial custom, thrice proclaimed, "*Le*

---

[1] M. Théophile Lavallée—Madame de Maintenon's most ardent apologist—wishes us to believe that she left the bedside of the king, when almost in the agonies of death, "for fear that the emotion caused by the sight of her tears might prejudice his health"!—Famille d'Aubigné, p. 468.

roi est mort;" and a faint response came back from a few bystanders in the courtyard below, "*Vive le roi!*"

Thus, in his seventy-seventh year, after the most eventful reign in French history—a reign of so much glory and so much obloquy—the great king went to his rest at last. "He had survived," says Saint Simon, "all his sons and grandsons, except the King of Spain. France had never seen a reign so long or a king so old."

CHAPTER XIV.

THE REGENT.

As if repenting at having given us this touching picture of the king's death, Saint Simon goes on to say, that excepting his valets, the Ministers, and Government officials—"in fact what may be called the *canaille* "— no one felt his loss. "Paris and the provinces breathed again, and leaped for joy. The people, ruined, overwhelmed, and desperate, gave thanks to God with a scandalous delight for a deliverance that exceeded their most ardent expectations." His body was carried to Saint Denis with the slightest possible pomp and ceremony; no tears were shed, and there was no public mourning.

The Parliament was summoned the next day; and the chamber was thronged by peers and councillors with anxious and expectant faces—the Duke of Maine among them, "bursting with joy," smiling and self-satisfied— while through the open doors were seen crowds of curious spectators and files of guards who had been ordered to line the avenues. The king's will was read, and then Orleans made a spirited speech in vindication of his rights — alluding with a marked emphasis to " those who had dared to make profit of the feebleness of a dying king." Fleury and D'Aguesseau eloquently supported him; and after a warm discussion, and an adjournment of the meeting, it ended (as Louis had himself foretold) in Orleans being declared Regent with full powers by a unanimous vote, while Maine was stripped of all authority, and every clause favourable to his claims found in the will was at once set aside. Even at this very meeting, when the future Government of the kingdom was at stake, Saint Simon's "small shrill voice" was heard protesting as to the rights of the dukes to remain covered when they addressed the Parliament (*affaire du bonnet*). "It was," he declared, "their most peculiar, most cherished, and most just prerogative!"

Public affairs during the king's minority were to be carried on by seven Councils — answering very much to our Public Departments, except that there was one of "Conscience" specially devoted to Church matters. Each council consisted of seven members; and above them all was that of the Regency, of which Saint Simon was himself a member. But these Councils had a brief existence, and within two years' time they were all abolished, with the exception of the Regent's select advisers.

Even more than either Alcibiades or Buckingham, the Regent was "all mankind's epitome." Two opposite natures seemed to be constantly struggling in him for the mastery, and his mother the Princess of Bavaria described this medley of good and evil in a well-known fable—"All the fairies had come to his birth, and each of them had given her son some talent, so that he possessed them all. But unluckily they had forgotten to invite one old fairy, who had disappeared for so long that no one had thought of her. She came at last, leaning on her little wand, after the others had each made her present to the child; and, growing more and more incensed at the neglect, she avenged herself by making all the talents given by the others absolutely worthless, and though he retained them all, none of them helped him in the least degree."[1] Saint Simon, who had known the Regent from boyhood, thoroughly confirms this character of him. He was an accomplished painter and musician, yet a drunken supper-party afforded the pleasantest sights and sounds to him; he had a taste for science and chemistry, yet would waste hours in foolish magical experiments; he had learning, eloquence, and a marvellous memory for facts and dates, yet surpassed even his own *roués*[2] of the Palais Royal in ribaldry and profanity; he was amiable, kind-hearted, and generous, yet "neither grace nor justice could be got from him except by working on his fears;" he was brave almost to rashness in the field, but was destitute of any moral courage, timid, irresolute, and incurably lazy in all matters except pleasure.

Louis knew his nephew's character as well as Saint Simon; and once, when Maréchal, his surgeon, was talking of Orleans's various accomplishments, and said that, if the prince had to work for his living, he would find five or six ways of getting it—"Yes," said Louis, "my nephew is all you have just said. He is a braggart

---

[1] Macaulay has applied this fable to Lord Byron's character in a well-known passage of his Essays.

[2] Orleans himself applied this word to his boon companions,—men who deserved to be "broken on the wheel"—or, as we might say, for whom hanging was too good.

of imaginary crimes" ("*c'est un fanfaron des crimes*"). I was quite amazed, says Saint Simon, at such a grand stroke of description coming from the king's mouth.

Saint Simon dwells at some length upon the mingled vein of superstition and scepticism in the character of Orleans, who was too clever, he says, to be an atheist, although he pretended to be one; and who, if a dangerous illness had attacked him, "would have thrown himself into the hands of all the priests and capuchins in Paris." But his great desire was "to raise the devil and make him speak," and for this purpose he would pass whole nights in the quarries of Vaugirard, uttering spells and invocations. Once while he was in this mood a clairvoyancer came to Paris, and brought with him a little girl who professed to see the future in a glass of water. Orleans invited them to the Palais Royal, and after testing the young girl's powers of prophecy with various questions, he at last asked her to describe what would happen at the king's death. (It should be noted that he told all this to Saint Simon in a conversation nine years before the king actually died.)

"She looked in the glass of water, and told him at some length all she saw. She accurately described the king's room at Versailles, and the furniture in it, precisely as it was when he died. She gave an exact picture of the king as he lay in his bed, and of everybody standing up close to the bed or in the room—a little child wearing a blue order, held in the arms of Madame de Ventadour—and at seeing her the girl uttered a cry of recognition, for she had seen her at Mademoiselle de Séry's. She then made them recognise Madame de Maintenon, and the singular figure of Fagon;[1]

---

[1] Fagon, the physician, was bent nearly double with age and rheumatism.

Madame the Duchess of Orleans, Madame la Duchesse, the Princess of Conti : she again cried out as she saw the Duke of Orleans—in a word, she made them recognise by her description all the princes and servants, the nobles and the valets, whom she saw around the bed. When she had told everything she saw, the Duke of Orleans, surprised that she had not described to them Monseigneur, or the Duke and the Duchess of Burgundy, or the Duke of Berry, asked her if she did not see figures of such and such an appearance. But she persistently declared that she did not, and described over again those that she actually did see. This is what the Duke of Orleans could not understand, and what astonished him extremely then as it did me, and we vainly sought to discover what it meant. The event explained it all. We were then in 1706. All these four princes were at that time full of life and health, and all four were dead before the king's death. It was the same with M. le Prince, M. le Duc, and with the Prince de Conti—none of whom the little girl saw in the glass, though she saw the children of the two last named, as well as M. du Maine, his children, and the Count of Toulouse. But, till the event took place, all this was left in obscurity.

"After thus satisfying his curiosity, the Duke of Orleans wished to know what his own fate was to be. But nothing more could be seen in the glass. Then the man, who was there, offered to show the Duke his own figure painted as it were upon the wall of the room, provided that he was not afraid of seeing it there ; and in about a quarter of an hour, after the man had gone through some gesticulations before them all, the figure of the Duke of Orleans, clothed as he was then and large as life, suddenly appeared upon the wall as though in a picture, with a crown upon his head. This crown was not that of France, nor that of Spain, nor that of England, nor that of any empire. The Duke, who gazed at it with all his eyes, could not divine its nature. He had never seen one like it. It had only four circles, and nothing on its summit. This crown covered the head of the figure.

"I take the opportunity [Saint Simon concludes] to show

from the obscurity of these two prophecies, the vanity of this sort of curiosity, the just deceit of the devil which God allows in order to punish the curiosity which He forbids—the clouds and darkness which result from it, in place of the light and satisfaction sought for. Orleans was then a long way from being Regent of the kingdom, or from even dreaming of such a thing! Yet this it was perhaps that this singular kind of crown announced to him. All this took place in Paris, at the house of his mistress, in presence of their most intimate circle of friends, on the very evening before the day on which he told me of it, and I thought the story so extraordinary that I have given it a place here,—not in the way of approval, but as a simple statement of fact."

Any virtuous instincts that Orleans might have originally possessed had been hopelessly perverted by the fatal influence of his tutor Dubois. This man had practised on the facile nature of his pupil, and instilled into his heart "an execrable poison." He taught him to disbelieve in the very existence of moral principle; to regard virtue and vice as mere conventional fictions dressed up by priests; that "honour in men and chastity in women were chimeras, and had no real existence in any one, except in a few poor slaves of prejudice," and that in his natural heart every man was vile and wicked. Orleans used occasionally to rally Saint Simon on his superior virtue, as being an old-fashioned complaint that he ought to have got over in his childhood; and he certainly did his best to show that he was not himself hampered by any such lingering sentiments of morality. "The more debauched a man was," we are told, "the more he esteemed him." His most outrageous orgies were purposely celebrated on the holiest days of the year, and his most familiar friends were selected from the most proficient graduates in vice. Their mean origin was rather a recommendation in his eyes, for he had a thorough contempt for nobles of his own rank,—in fact, he thought they were, if possible, more easily bought and sold than the rest of mankind; and he was disposed to agree with his mistress, Madame de Sabran, who declared that "God at the creation had taken what was left of the clay, and made of it the souls of princes and lackeys."

But Orleans was something more than a man of pleasure. Up till five o'clock in the day he was the Regent, and, as such, devoted himself to public business. He presided at his council, consulted with his colleagues, dictated to his secretaries, received ambassadors; at two o'clock he took his chocolate, for he never dined, and then paid visits or entertained visitors up till five. After that hour he considered himself absolved from official cares, and rushed off like an emancipated schoolboy to the Luxembourg or Palais Royal, where he amused himself for the rest of the evening. "I was never present," says Saint Simon, "at one of his suppers. . . . They were scenes of unbridled licence; and when the guests were very drunk and had made a good deal of noise, they went to bed, to begin the same game again the next day." Yet in his wildest moments Orleans never let a State secret escape him, and the most favoured of his mistresses was never admitted to his confidence. He treated them all, we are told, just as they deserved to be treated—giving them little power and very little money. Whatever the Regent's follies might have been, he was not to be too easily duped by a Maintenon or a Pompadour.

One generous act of the Regent, in the early days of his power, deserves to be recorded. He sent for the list of all the *lettres de cachet* issued during the last reign—the number has been computed at something like thirty thousand—went carefully through the names of those imprisoned in the Bastille, and restored them all to liberty, excepting such as were charged with treason or grave offences.

Among the poor wretches thus set free was one unhappy man who had come from Italy, an entire stranger to France, some thirty years before, and who had been arrested by the police the moment he set foot in Paris, and thrown into the Bastille. No one knew his offence; no record of any crime appeared against him in the prison books; and the officials themselves believed "it was a mistake."

"When his liberty was announced to him, he sadly asked what he could do with it. He had not, he said, a farthing in the world—he did not know a soul in Paris—not even the name of a single street, nor a person in all France. His relations were probably dead, and his property divided among strangers, during his long absence. He did not know what he could do with himself if set free, and he begged to be allowed to remain in the Bastille for the rest of his days, with food and lodging. This favour was granted him."

Orleans would also have recalled the Huguenots, and repaired, if he could, some of the mischief caused by that signal act of tyranny which had banished them from France. But, strange to say, Saint Simon strongly opposed such a measure—though on political, not on religious, grounds. There would be another League, he declared, and probably another civil war, if these exiles were allowed to return.

The embarrassed state of the finances was the chief

difficulty with which the Regent had to deal. The national debt amounted to more than £120,000,000 in English money, while there was not more than £30,000 of available cash in the Treasury. Various expedients for raising money were adopted. An edict was passed to control and liquidate some of the floating debt: a Chamber of Finance was appointed, and the capitalists had to disgorge part of their gains; and then the value of the gold louis was raised, and the coinage practically debased. When matters seemed most hopeless, a Scotchman, named Law, proposed a highly tempting scheme to the Regent. Without tax, without additional expense, without trouble or danger to any one, money, he declared, was to double itself and circulate rapidly through the country, by the simple expedient of putting it into his bank, and receiving the equivalent in paper notes. The Regent caught at the idea: a National Bank was established, and shares in it were eagerly sought for, while the paper notes issued by it at once rose to a premium.

But, as Saint Simon sagaciously asked, how was this paper currency to be regulated? Such a system as Law's might answer in a limited monarchy: but France was not like England; and "the expense of a war, the rapacity of a Minister, a favourite, or a mistress, would soon exhaust the bank, and ruin the holders of notes." Nor did the Parliament view the scheme with any favour. They refused to ratify the Regent's edict, which authorised the purchase of Law's bank by the State; and they even threatened to hang Law himself in front of the Palais de Justice. But their remonstrances were quietly overruled.

In 1717, Law started the Mississippi Company—as

wild and illusory a scheme as the South Sea Bubble itself. Magnificent promises were held out to the shareholders — unlimited wealth from the gold-mines of Louisiana, and a monopoly of French commerce. The shares at once went up to twenty times their value; enormous fortunes were made in a few hours; paper notes were issued in ceaseless abundance; and Law's offices, in the narrow Rue de Quincampoix, were thronged night and day by eager speculators. "He lived in a state of siege," says Saint Simon, "and saw people clamber in through his windows from the garden, or drop down the chimney into his private room. Men only talked of millions."

Saint Simon himself was sceptical both as to the bank and the company, and he refused to take a share in either one or the other. "Since the days of Midas," he said, "no one before this Scotchman had ever been gifted with the power of turning what he touched into gold; and this skilful jugglery, which put Peter's money into Paul's pocket, must, sooner or later, end in utter ruin." It was even as he anticipated. The foolish prodigality of the Regent, and the extravagant amount of paper-money issued by Law, produced their natural consequences. There was a vague suspicion, a panic, a run upon the bank; the Prince of Conti alone carried off three waggon-loads of gold, instead of paper, in an afternoon: then every one tried to realise money in place of his notes before the crash came—and then the bubble burst. In spite of every effort made by the Regent to bolster up the system, even going so far as to confiscate all the gold and jewellery found in private houses, Law's notes were found to be waste paper; eighty thousand families were ruined, and, amidst the general distress and consternation, Law himself escaped from France.

Strangely enough, Saint Simon does not blame this adventurer. "There was neither avarice nor roguery in his composition," he tells us. "He was the dupe of his own Mississippi scheme. . . . He reasoned like an Englishman—not knowing how opposed to the spirit of commerce is the frivolity of the French nation, their inexperience, and their greediness to enrich themselves by one lucky stroke."

It may be doubted if Saint Simon played quite the important part under the Regency that he had pictured to himself. He was, no doubt, one of Orleans's oldest and most trusted friends; but then Orleans was keen-sighted and suspicious to the last degree. He only laughed at Saint Simon's warmth and impetuosity; he ridiculed the pretensions of "the dukes;" he turned off the most serious questions with some buffoonery; and, if he could not otherwise escape, he trifled and temporised, or made promises that were never kept.

But, in spite of many disappointments, Saint Simon enjoyed some days of signal triumph; and among them may be reckoned that on which the Regent was at last persuaded to take heart of grace, summon a Bed of Justice, and "humble the arrogance of the Parliament, and strip the false plumage from the king's bastard children."

Maine, whose degradation was the special object of this Bed of Justice, seems to have offered a passive resistance; but his wife showed more spirit than her husband, and declared she would set fire to the four corners of the kingdom sooner than give up his rights.

She was an imperious, self-willed, fantastic little personage—small in stature, like all the Condés, but with a restless and volatile temperament. She reigned at Sceaux like a queen of Lilliput, giving endless *fêtes* and entertainments—now acting "Athalie," and now studying astronomy or reading Greek with the "learned Malezieux." She turned the night into day, and spent her husband's money in the most reckless fashion. "But he never dared say a word," says Saint Simon, "for fear of her going quite mad; as it was, she was more than half crazed."

For the present, however, she gave up her pleasures to search all the old chronicles she could find to prove from history that the natural sons of kings were as good as princes of the blood-royal; and Madame de Staal tells us how she found the Duchess half buried under a pile of huge folios, "like Enceladus under Etna," and how laboriously she examined them with the assistance of some distinguished antiquaries. But, as her friend observes, these *savants* probably knew more about the customs of the Chaldeans than of the Court of Versailles, and precedents taken from the family of Nimrod would scarcely apply to the family of Louis XIV.

But all the antiquaries in the world could not have averted the inevitable humiliation of Maine. His enemy, Saint Simon, had been working night and day, arranging the details of the Bed of Justice where the sentence of degradation was to be formally pronounced; and he tells us of "the rosy thoughts,"—"the sweet and unalloyed delight of the prospect."

At last the fatal day dawned, "so immeasurably and

perseveringly desired," when the insults and indignities of a lifetime were to be wiped away in one supreme hour of revenge. Every step had been taken to guard against the possibility of resistance. The household troops were under arms, and the approaches to the Tuileries were lined by Swiss guards and musketeers. The Regent's Council met, and without even putting the question to the vote, two decrees were read—the first annulling a recent enactment of the Parliament on a question of finance, and the second depriving Maine of his rank and honours as a prince, and reducing him to the position of a simple duke. And then the Parliament were summoned in their turn to hear these sentences of humiliation. Saint Simon feasted his eyes on the spectacle of their astonishment and impotent indignation.

"This was the moment when I relished, with a delight utterly impossible to express in words, the sight of these haughty legislators, who had dared to refuse us the salutation, prostrate on their knees, and rendering at our feet a homage to the throne, while we (the peers) were seated, with our heads covered, at the side of the same throne. It is this situation and these postures that alone plead, with the most piercing evidence, the cause of those who, in very truth and reality, are the king's right-hand men (*laterales regis*), and opposed to these representatives (*vas electum*) of the Third Estate. My eyes, fixed and glued upon these haughty *bourgeois*, scanned all these grand gentlemen of the bar, as they knelt or stood, with the ample folds of their fur robes—paltry rabbits' fur, that tried to imitate ermine—swaying to and fro at each long and redoubled genuflexion, that only ceased when the king gave his orders through the Keeper of the Seals, and these heads uncovered and humiliated on a level with our feet.

"When the President of Parliament had finished his remonstrances, the Keeper of the Seals ascended the steps to the throne, and then, without asking further advice, returned to his place, looked at the President, and said, '*The king wishes to be obeyed, and to be obeyed at once.*' This grand speech was a thunder-stroke that confounded the presidents and councillors in the most wonderful way. They all bowed their heads, and it was long before the majority raised them again."

But there was even a greater triumph to come. The second decree, which placed Maine at the bottom of the list of dukes, and deprived him of all his privileges, including his office of governor to the king, was read and registered, to the consternation of his friends.

"The Chief President, stunned by the last blow, made such a surprisingly long face, that I thought his chin had fallen on his knees. . . . But all the while I was myself dying of joy. I was so oppressed that I feared I should faint: my heart, dilated to excess, found no room to beat. The violence I did myself in order to let nothing escape me was infinite; yet nevertheless this torment was delicious. I compared the years and time of my servitude,—those hateful days when, dragged like a victim at the wheels of the Parliament, I had so many times adorned the triumph of the bastards—those various degrees by which they had mounted to this height above our heads,—I compared them, I say, to this court of justice and of arbitration—to this their frightful disgrace, which, at the same time, raised us, the peers, by the force of the counter-shock. . . . I thanked and congratulated myself that it was through ME that all this had been done. I thought of the dazzling splendour of such a revenge in the presence of the king and so august an assemblage. I was triumphant,—I was avenging myself,—I swam in the delights of vengeance. I enjoyed to the full the accomplishment of the most ardent and most continuous desires of my life."

The Duke of Maine bore his humiliation with his usual coolness; but the Duchess was furious when she heard of it. "All that is left me is the disgrace of having married you," she said bitterly to her husband; and when ordered to give up her rooms at the Tuileries, in her passion she broke the windows, the china, and everything she could lay her hands on. Then, to revenge herself, she engaged in a foolish conspiracy with Spain to depose the Regent. Her letters were intercepted, and both she and her husband, with many of their friends, were arrested and imprisoned for some months, until Orleans, with his careless good-nature, released and forgave them all.

Paris received an illustrious visitor in 1717—the Czar, Peter the Great. Saint Simon, who "stared at him for an hour, without taking his eyes off him," was much impressed by his commanding presence and "unmistakable air of greatness," although he notices the curious spasm that every now and then distorted his face and gave him "a wild and terrible look." Everything was done by the Regent to entertain his imperial guest. Splendid rooms were prepared for him at the Louvre, which, however, the Czar found too splendid for comfort: there was a parade of the household troops; a hunt at Fontainebleau; a Court ball, and a grand opera, where the Czar scandalised the audience by calling for beer, and drinking it in the royal box. He was impatient of State ceremonies, and liked nothing better than to wander about Paris unattended, talk to the workmen employed on the revolving bridge, taste the soldiers' soup at the Invalides, and drive from one end of the town to the other in a hackney-coach. If we may believe Saint

Simon, he showed himself a true Russian in his taste for strong liquors. He drank a bottle or two of beer, and the same quantity of wine, at dinner, and "a quart of brandy afterwards, by way of liqueur." His suite ate and drank even more than their master; and the chaplain, like a worthy son of the Church, "consumed half as much again as the rest of the suite." In other respects, their filthy habits made them as unwelcome visitors in Paris as afterwards at Evelyn's house at Deptford.

After a visit of six weeks, the Czar left Paris, greatly delighted with all he had seen, but much troubled in mind by the excessive luxury of the Court, which he prophesied must, sooner or later, bring ruin on the country.

CHAPTER XV.

CARDINAL DUBOIS.

It was Saint Simon's fate, up to the last hour of his political life, to be thwarted and overruled by the man whom, of all others, his soul most abhorred, yet who was not only the most able politician of his day, but had considerably more influence with the Regent than Saint Simon himself: in fact, he had made himself "his master's master." His other biographers (Capefigue alone excepted) represent Dubois as having been, in actual life, much what he is said to be in these Memoirs— "soft, supple, cringing, a flatterer and false admirer, . . . with falsehood written on his brow; immeasurably depraved in morals, . . . despising and deriding good faith, honour, probity, and truth."[1]

So much may be granted; but when Saint Simon says that "he was destitute of all talent," and that "his

---

[1] One evening, when the Prince Regent was dining at Holland House, the conversation turned upon the question as to who was the wickedest man that ever lived. "The Regent Orleans, and he was a *prince*," said Sydney Smith, looking at the Prince Regent. "I should have given the preference to his tutor, the Abbé Dubois, and he was a *priest*, Mr Sydney," was the quiet rebuke of his Royal Highness.

capacity was *nil*," it is clear that in this case, as in other instances, he has failed to distinguish between the moral and intellectual qualities of the enemy whom he thus mercilessly assails. The abilities of Dubois are as notorious as his profligacy. He had considerable humour, learning, and knowledge of men and books; a taste for letters and science; great powers of application; and had shown singular firmness and dexterity in his defeat of Cellamare's conspiracy, and in the negotiations which resulted in the Quadruple Alliance. But this triumph of diplomacy was an additional crime in Saint Simon's eyes. He was himself a Jacobite at heart, and it was with bitter indignation that he saw the Regent sacrifice the Stuart cause which Louis XIV. would never give up, even in his heaviest reverses, while the unfortunate son of James II. had a price put upon his head, and was forced to seek an asylum in Rome.[1] Saint Simon fretted and fumed at this English alliance. Both Dubois and the Regent, he declared, were "too much the humble servants of the house of Hanover;" but he accounts for their apostasy from the traditional policy of France by the "Anglomania" of the prince, and the heavy annual pension paid by the English Cabinet to the Minister.

"Every ecclesiastic," says Saint Simon, "who once succeeds in getting a footing in the government of his country—however base his origin—makes it his sole object in life to become a Cardinal, and is ready to sacrifice everything unreservedly to this end." Dubois

[1] There are two letters preserved among the manuscripts in the British Museum from "Jacques, Roy," to "my cousin, the Duke of Saint Simon," dated from Albano in 1721.

soon began to mount the steps of this ladder, and one morning he told the Regent that he had just had "a pleasant dream of being Archbishop of Cambray,"—the see being then vacant. Even Orleans was scandalised at the proposal, for, putting aside the question of his profligate life, Dubois was not even in holy orders. "Make a scoundrel like you archbishop! Where will you find another scoundrel who will consecrate you?" Dubois assured him that there would be no difficulty—in fact, the man was in the next room: his own chaplain, the Archbishop of Rheims, would do all that was necessary. The Regent reluctantly gave his consent, and Dubois was ordained deacon and priest at the same service, and shortly afterwards he was actually consecrated archbishop.

He showed no false modesty on the occasion; and when one of his colleagues sneered at the appointment with what Saint Simon calls "pathetic malignity," Dubois justified himself by the precedent of Saint Ambrose, who had been consecrated archbishop even before he was baptised. "I was so horror-stricken at such profanity," says Saint Simon, "that I rushed to the door of the room, that I might hear no more." He implored Orleans, by all that was most sacred, not to attend the consecration, as it would be a mockery to God and an insult to the Church; and Orleans faithfully promised that nothing should induce him to be present. But the first thing Saint Simon heard the next morning was that the Regent had set off in full state, with his usual escort, for the church where the consecration was to take place. One of his mistresses had persuaded him to change his mind even in that short interval.

Once made archbishop, Dubois began to move heaven and earth to obtain a cardinal's hat. He entreated, promised, and bribed in all directions, even getting the Pretender, as well as George I., to support his claims. The Regent, with his usual inconsistency, first declared "he would throw the little impudent rascal into the lowest dungeon if he should venture even to think of such a thing," and the next day told Torcy to write to Rome in Dubois's favour.

Fortunately for the Regent's candidate, the new Pope, Innocent XIII., happened to be a Frenchman (Conti); and in 1721, after expending an incredible sum in bribes, Dubois was at last made happy with the red hat; but, as he complacently said, "what he valued far more than the Roman purple was the *empressement* shown by all the European sovereigns in procuring it for him."

If we may believe Saint Simon, Dubois's new dignity as a prince of the Church made not the least difference in his manners or language.

"One morning he could not find something he wanted, and began to rage and swear at his clerks, saying, that if there were not enough of them, he would engage forty or fifty or a hundred more, and making the most frightful noise. His secretary, Verrier, listened to him tranquilly, and the Cardinal asked him if it was not a horrible thing to be so badly used, considering the expense he had been put to; and then he flew into a fresh fit of passion, and insisted upon Verrier's answering him.

"'Monseigneur,' said Verrier, 'take one more clerk, and let his only employment be to swear and storm for you, and all will go well. You will have much more time for other matters, and you will be much better served.'

"The Cardinal began to laugh, and was appeased."

We may select one more out of the many anecdotes which Saint Simon tells us of Dubois, and then we may leave his Eminence.

Madame de Conflans, governess to the Regent's children, was persuaded, much against her will, that she ought to pay a complimentary visit to Dubois on his new accession of dignity.

"She arrived at Versailles just as people were leaving dinner, and was shown into a large room where there were eight or ten persons waiting to speak to the Cardinal, who was standing near the fireplace with some woman, to whom he was giving a taste of the rough side of his tongue. Fear seized Madame de Conflans, who was but small, and looked even smaller than she was. Still, she timidly approached as this woman retired. The Cardinal, seeing her advance, asked her sharply what she wanted.

"'Monseigneur!' said she; 'oh, Monseigneur——

"'Monseigneur!' interrupted the Cardinal; 'come, it can't be done.'

"'But, Monseigneur——' she said again.

"'By all that's infernal!' interrupted the Cardinal again, 'I tell you once more, as I told you just now, it can't be done.'

"'Monseigneur——' Madame de Conflans began again, wishing to explain that she wanted nothing; but at this word the Cardinal seized her by the shoulders, twirled her round, gave her a thump on the back, and pushed her out.

"'Go to the devil!' said he, 'and leave me in peace.'

"She thought she should have fallen flat on the ground, and rushed away in a fury, shedding hot tears, and arrived in this state at the Duchess of Orleans's house, to whom she told her story as well as her sobs would allow her.

"People were so accustomed to these wild freaks of the Cardinal, and this was thought so singular and amusing, that the recital of it caused shouts of laughter, which completely crushed the poor Conflans, who made a solemn vow she would never again set foot inside this madman's house."

In 1721, two marriages were arranged to cement the alliance between France and Spain. The young king was betrothed to the Infanta (then of the mature age of three); and the Prince of the Asturias, the heir-apparent of Spain, was to marry the Regent's daughter, Mdlle. de Montpensier. A special ambassador was to be sent on the occasion, to demand formally the hand of the Infanta and to sign the marriage-contract; and Saint Simon easily persuaded Orleans to nominate him for this important mission. His only object in going, he is careful to add, was to secure the rank of Grandee for his second son, and possibly the order of the Golden Fleece for the eldest. "I so thought to do a good stroke of business for my family, and to return home in great content."

His journey, which took him about three weeks, is described with his usual humour and vivacity; and from the moment he crossed the frontiers he seems to have got rid of his care and discontent. "As I crossed the Pyrenees," he says, "I left with France the rain and bad weather, and found a pure sky and a charming temperature, with scenery and views changing every moment." As he went on, "all seemed flowers and fruits." For once in his life he found himself appreciated at what he considered his proper value, and it is with evidently gratified vanity that he tells us how he was *fêted* on his progress from town to town; how he was received with enthusiasm by the populace of Madrid, and "almost stifled with compliments" by the Spanish grandees; how he went to Court in a State carriage drawn by eight horses, with twenty-five other coaches following his own; with what dignity he advanced up the long Hall of Mirrors; and with what a stately grace Philip V. announced his satisfaction at the marriage, " using such a marvellously judicious choice of words and expressions, that I thought I heard that grand master of ceremonies, the late king [Louis XIV.], himself addressing me."

Madrid was illuminated, a State ball was given in honour of the occasion, and Saint Simon, who seems to have amused that solemn Court by his vivacity and sprightliness, received the royal command to dance. He tells us that, though he had not danced for thirty years and had a heavy coat on, he bore himself bravely in minuet and quadrille; and that he was refreshed, after his exertions (like Mr Pepys) " by a glass of excellent neat wine."

Their Catholic Majesties also commanded his attendance at a royal battue, where the game included almost every four-footed creature, from wild-boars to polecats. Saint Simon's own contribution would scarcely have been a matter of congratulation to a modern sportsman. " I shot a fox," he says complacently, " a little before the proper time ;" by which he means that the Crown-Prince, who was in the same *cache*, ought to have had the chance of shooting the fox first,— for at the battue, as everywhere else, royalty took precedence.

Then he visited the Escurial, where he showed such insatiable curiosity, and asked so many embarrassing questions, that one of the monks in charge completely lost his temper.

"And so we did the round of the mortuary chamber, talking over and discussing all we saw. As we passed to the further end of the room, the coffin of the unhappy Don Carlos met our view.

"'As for him,' said I, 'it is well known how and why *he* died.'

"At this speech the fat monk stammered, and maintained that he had died from natural causes, and began to declaim against the stories which he said had been spread about his death. I only smiled, and said I allowed it was not true that he had died by having his veins opened. These words completed the irritation of the monk, who began to babble in a sort of fury. At first I amused myself by listening in silence, and then I remarked that the king, soon after his arrival in Spain, had the curiosity to have the coffin of Don Carlos opened, and that I had been told by a man who was present (it was Louville), the prince's head had been found between his legs, and that his father, Philip II., had caused him to be beheaded in prison in his own presence.

"'Very well!' cried the monk, in a furious passion; 'apparently it was because Don Carlos had thoroughly deserved his fate, for Philip II. had permission from the Pope to do it.' And then he began to extol with all his might the marvellous piety and justice of Philip II., and the boundless power of the Pope, and denounced the heresy of the man who doubted that his Holiness had not the power to ordain, decide, and dispose of all as he chose.

"Such is the fanaticism of countries under the Inquisition, where learning is a crime, and where ignorance and superstition are the cardinal virtues. Although my official character would have protected me, I did not choose to dispute or have a ridiculous scene with this *piffre* of a monk. I contented myself with laughing, and making signs to those who were with me to keep silence. So the monk said all he liked at his leisure, and went on a long while without being able to check his passion. Perhaps he perceived by our faces that we were laughing at him, though without words or gestures. At last he showed us the rest of the chamber, still fuming with rage, and then we descended to the Pantheon."

Saint Simon's visit to the Escurial was disagreeably interrupted by an attack of the small-pox, which laid him up there for more than six weeks. He was, however, carefully nursed and attended by the King of Spain's physician (a "M. Higgins"), and his recovery was complete. He recommends "broth made of beef and partridge, with a little Rota wine," as an excellent diet during convalescence.

On his return to Madrid he found everything in readiness for the marriage of the Prince of the Asturias with the Regent's daughter, who had arrived at the Spanish Court. Cardinal Borgia had been sent from Rome expressly to officiate, and the ceremony was to take place in a private chapel of the palace. Saint Simon happened to be one of the first to arrive on the scene.

"Cardinal Borgia, in his pontifical robes, stood at a corner of the reading-desk, with his face turned towards me, learning his lesson between two chaplains in surplices, who held a large book open before him. The good prelate did not know how to read in it; he made an effort, read in a high voice, and all wrong. His chaplains took him up; he got angry and grumbled at them; began again, and was again corrected, and got more and more angry, until at last he turned round and shook them by their surplices. I laughed to my heart's content, for he saw nothing—he was so occupied and perplexed by his lesson.

"Then the king, the queen, the prince, and the princesses arrived, with all the Court, and their arrival was announced in a loud tone. 'Let them wait!' cried the Cardinal in a fury; 'I am not ready.' In fact, they were obliged to wait while he went on with his lesson, with his face redder than his hat, and all the time in a furious passion."

However, Cardinal Borgia, with the assistance of the chaplains, at last succeeded in getting through the marriage service; and when the ceremony was over, Saint Simon was made happy even beyond his utmost hopes. Both he and his second son were raised to the rank of Spanish grandees of the first class, and his eldest son (the Vidame de Chartres) was invested with the Golden Fleece at a long and stately ceremonial that delighted his father's heart; the king himself giving the *accolade* with the sword of the founder and grand-captain of the Order, Don Gonzalo de Cordova. Then followed the usual marriage festivities,—banquets, illuminations, torch-races, and naval combats; and after a six months' visit, Saint Simon left Madrid highly delighted both with Spain and the Spaniards, and especially pleased at having so nobly "branched" his family.

Soon after his return to Versailles a violent scene took place between Cardinal Dubois and Marshal Villeroy, the young king's governor. The Marshal was clearly the aggressor in this quarrel. On some slight provocation he had stormed and threatened, and made such an uproar, that he was almost dragged out of the room by Cardinal Bissy, who was the only witness of this extraordinary interview. Dubois himself rushed off at once to the Regent's cabinet, and burst into the room, where the prince was talking with Saint Simon, "like a whirlwind, with his eyes starting from his head," and scarcely able to articulate between rage and fear. He put it plainly to the Regent that he must choose once for all between himself and Villeroy, for, after what had passed, they could not both remain at Versailles. Orleans in this case did not take long to make up his mind. He had been provoked more than once by the insolent acts of Villeroy, and the very next morning the Marshal was arrested, and after "exhaling his anger," as Saint Simon calls it, in his own chateau, he was sent into honourable banishment as governor of Lyons.

Thenceforward Dubois had nothing between himself and the highest office in the State, and in little more than a week after the disappearance of Villeroy he was formally named Prime Minister by the Regent. This evil day had long been foreseen and dreaded by Saint Simon. Sooner or later he had felt certain that Dubois would engross the supreme power, and would be to the Regent what the Mayors of the Palace had been to the *rois fainéants* of earlier history; and he had watched Orleans drifting hopelessly and helplessly to this inevitable end. Orleans had himself foreseen it, had dreaded it like Saint Simon, and yet, in his "incurable feebleness," could not or would not make the slightest effort to save himself. One morning he had been complaining with unusual bitterness of the void he felt in his life, of his indifference to the pleasures of wine and love, and of his weariness of State affairs; and then Saint Simon broke the silence he had maintained for years as to the Regent's private life, and made the last, the strongest, and perhaps the most eloquent of all his appeals to the friend of his boyhood—urging him to dismiss his *roués* and his mistresses, to give up his notorious suppers at the Palais Royal, to do justice to his natural abilities, and above all, not to enslave himself to a Prime Minister. Orleans listened in silence and embarrassment.

"Then he sat up straight on his chair. 'Ah, well!' said he, 'I will go and plant my cabbages at Villars-Cotterets.'

Then he got up and began to walk about the room, and I with him.

* * * * *

"Finding himself near the wall, at the corner of his desk where there were two chairs (I still see where they were standing), he drew me by the arm towards one of them, while he set himself down upon the other, and then, turning completely round to face me, asked me sharply if I did not remember to have seen Dubois valet to Saint Laurent, and thinking himself then only too fortunate to be that; and then he enumerated all the different steps and stages of the Cardinal's fortunes up to that very moment, and then he exclaimed—

"'And yet he is not content. He persecutes me to get himself declared Prime Minister; and I am perfectly certain that, even when he is that, still he will not be content; and what the devil can he be after that?'

"And then, all at once, he answered his own question, murmuring to himself—'*Se faire Dieu le Père,*—if he can.'

"'Oh, most assuredly,' said I; 'it is just the very thing we may be quite certain he will do. It is for you, sir, who know him so well, to see if you are well advised to make yourself his footstool for him to step over your head.'

"'Oh, I will take good care to stop his doing that,' he answered; and then he began to walk about the room again afresh."

The next day this conversation was renewed on the same subject—Saint Simon being vehement and eloquent, as usual, against the very idea of a Prime Minister, and Orleans listening gloomily and patiently as before

"A long silence followed my strong protest. The Duke's head, supported by his hands, had by degrees sunk almost on his desk. He raised it at last, looked at me with a sullen and desponding air, and then lowered his eyes, which seemed to me full of shame, and still remained some time seated as he was. At last he rose and took several turns about the room, still saying nothing. But what was my astonishment and confusion when he at last broke his silence, stopped short, turned half towards me without raising his eyes, and said all at once in a sad low voice—

"'We must stop all this. I must declare him Prime Minister almost immediately.'

"'Sir,' said I, 'you are wise and good, and, above all—the master. Have you any commands to give me for Meudon?'

"I abruptly made him a reverence, and was leaving the room, when he called out, 'But I shall see you again soon, shall I not?' I made no reply, and closed the door.

"The faithful and patient Belle Ile was still waiting outside, and had stayed in the same place where I had left him, at the entrance, for two mortal hours, without counting the time that he had waited before my arrival.[1] He caught hold of me as soon as he saw me, and earnestly whispered in my ear, 'Eh, well! how do we stand?'

"'Nothing can be better,' I answered, restraining myself as well as I could. 'I regard the matter as settled, and it is on the point of being declared.'

"'That is too delightful,' said he. 'I must go at once and relieve our friend's anxiety.'

"I gave him no message, but hastened to get rid of him and be in peace at Meudon, and exhale my indignation at my ease."

The very next day Saint Simon called on Dubois to compliment him on being Prime Minister, and was warmly thanked for his disinterested friendship, and for having so successfully advocated his claims! "I was not deceived by all this," says Saint Simon, "for I saw clearly that he only wanted to throw the odium of

---

[1] Belle Ile was the confidant of Dubois, and was in this case, Saint Simon thinks, acting as his spy. It was fortunate that he could not hear or see through the doors of the cabinet.

his promotion on my shoulders." Possibly Saint Simon thought that all was fair in war against such an adversary; but his double-dealing and hypocrisy (to use the mildest terms for it) are strangely at variance with the frank outspoken honesty that he so often claims to be the distinctive mark of his character. But it may have been, as M. Chéruel suggests, that he had himself unconsciously deteriorated in the demoralising atmosphere of the Regency.

Cardinal Dubois, however, did not live long to enjoy either his honours or his wealth, computed at £40,000 a-year in our money. In the following year (1723) he underwent a painful operation, and died miserably after it,—refusing to receive the Sacrament, and "gnashing his teeth at his surgeons, in the greatest rage and despair at having to give up his life."

"What a monster of fortune," Saint Simon goes on, "and from what a low origin he sprang, and how suddenly and fearfully he was cast down! Truly to him might be applied the words of the Psalmist: 'I have seen the wicked man exalted like the cedars of Lebanon: I passed by, and lo! he was gone, and his place could nowhere be found.'"

CHAPTER XVI.

SAINT SIMON IN RETIREMENT.

SAINT SIMON took no part in public affairs after that strange interview with the Regent described in the last chapter. He felt that his day, such as it was, had gone by,—that the times were out of joint for him. Many of his old friends were dead; others were estranged; he was slighted by the younger generation; and as for Orleans himself, repugnance, he tells us, began to be mingled with the pity he felt for this poor prince. The disorder that took place at the consecration of the king in 1722 was a sign to him of still worse things that were to follow. Rank and precedence, he says, were utterly disregarded; the nobility were excluded from their proper dignities; the complete re-establishment of "the bastards" was evidently near at hand. And thus, seeing nothing but humiliation and annoyance in what was passing round him, Saint Simon goes back to the past, and dwells at some length on the career of his brother-in-law, Lauzun, whose life had been a succession of marvellous adventures. He dwells upon it, he says, for a special reason :—

"Another feeling has prolonged my recital. I am drawing near a term I fear to touch, because my desires cannot be in harmony with the truth: they are ardent, and in consequence bitterly painful, because the other sentiment is terrible, and leaves not the least room for any possible palliation. The terror of arriving at this term has stopped me short, has arrested my hand, has frozen my blood.

"It will be seen at once that I am about to speak of the death, and the *manner* of the death, of the Duke of Orleans; and after such a tender and long attachment between us— for it lasted all his life, and will last all my life—the terrible story of his death has pierced my heart with terror and sorrow for him. It makes me shudder to my very marrow with the horror of the thought that God, in His anger, granted his prayer that he might die suddenly."

The Regent's health had been hopelessly shattered by the excesses of thirty years; and one morning Saint Simon (who rarely saw him in these latter days) was horrified to see the change that had come over him. His face was flushed almost purple, his air was dull and heavy, and his utterance was so thick that he could scarcely articulate. It was the beginning of the end. A few days afterwards, while Orleans was talking to one of his mistresses, he suddenly fell backwards in an apoplectic fit, and never recovered either his speech or consciousness. Before Saint Simon could reach Versailles the Regent was dead, and with his death these Memoirs come to an appropriate conclusion.

Saint Simon both feared and distrusted the Duke of Bourbon, who now became Prime Minister; and of Cardinal Fleury — the young king's tutor — who succeeded Bourbon, he speaks with all his accustomed bitterness. "This prelate," he tells us, "concealed under his apparent modesty and gentleness a sublimely ungrateful, vainglorious, and revengeful heart." It was not long before he received a polite hint from Fleury that his presence at Versailles would be dispensed with. "Very little was wanting," he says, "to confirm me in taking the course I had long ago decided on. I went to Paris with the firm resolution of not appearing before the new masters of the kingdom, except on those rare occasions when I should be obliged to pay the indispensable visits of ceremony." For the remainder of his life he divided his time between his town house in the Rue St Dominique and his country chateau. Troubles came thickly upon him in his later years. In 1743 he lost his wife—"that pearl of inestimable price," as he calls her; and a few years afterwards he lost his eldest son, the Duke of Ruffec. His only daughter, who was deformed and repulsively ugly, had made an unhappy marriage: his second son was hopelessly ill of an incurable disease. Meanwhile his own affairs grew more and more involved, and his debts at last amounted to upwards of £60,000.

Beyond these sad facts of his family history, and occasional references in the songs and pasquinades of the day, we know scarcely anything of Saint Simon's private life, except that he read and wrote perpetually, —finding, perhaps, as others have done before and since, greater satisfaction and content among his books and papers than had ever fallen to his lot as a councillor or politician; and finding also a secret and increasing pleasure in recording all that he had seen and suffered, and in making his final appeal to posterity to judge between him and his enemies.

How busily he was occupied in these years of enforced retirement is shown by the voluminous manuscripts he has left behind him; and it is clear that he spared neither time nor labour in his historical researches, consulting both men and books, and (as has been said) annotating Dangeau's Memoirs, in order to verify his facts and dates. Among his countless portfolios of essays and treatises there are two of especial interest. One is the "*Paquet d'Espagne,*" on which M. Drumont is now at work; and the other bears the whimsical title of "*Cendres que j'ai vues à plusieurs depuis* 1723," which M. Baschet thinks may possibly turn out to be the promised continuation of his Memoirs up to the death of Cardinal Fleury.

Saint Simon died at the age of eighty in his house at Paris, and was buried—as he had expressly desired—by the side of his wife in the crypt of the parish church of La Ferté Vidame. But in 1794 a party of red Republicans tore the bodies from their coffins, and threw them into a common trench outside the churchyard; and thus, as it were by the irony of fate, the proud Duke, who in his lifetime had regarded even the *bourgeois* as beneath his notice, was destined after his death to share a grave with the vilest of the vile.

END OF SAINT SIMON.

www.ingramcontent.com/pod-product-compliance
Lightning Source LLC
Chambersburg PA
CBHW021835230426
43669CB00008B/982